From personal finances to stock trading, *The Neatest Little Guide to Do-It-Yourself Investing* provides you with the in-depth information and guidance you need to come out financially ahead.

You'll discover:

- How to think like an investor
- How to implement the simplest investment plan ever
- Why investing for the long term pays off
- How to avoid "loss aversion"
- How to set and meet your financial goals
- The importance of investment research
- Kelly's Heroes—7 stock tips for your recovery portfolio

...and much more!

Jason Kelly created the *Neatest Little Guide* series to make personal money management easy for everyone. This is the fifth book in the series, preceded by *Mutual Fund Investing*, *Stock Market Investing*, *Personal Finance*, and *Making Money Online*. Jason teaches financial seminars throughout California and publishes *The NeatSheet*, a monthly investment newsletter. You can reach him online at *www.jasonkelly.com*, where you'll find current columns, book updates, and a slew of investment tools. He lives in Los Angeles.

Also by Jason Kelly

NONFICTION
The Neatest Little Guide to Mutual Fund Investing
The Neatest Little Guide to Stock Market Investing
The Neatest Little Guide to Personal Finance
The Neatest Little Guide to Making Money Online

FICTION
Y2K—It's Already Too Late

The Neatest Little Guide to Do-It-Yourself Investing

JASON KELLY

A PLUME BOOK

PLUME
Published by the Penguin Group
Penguin Putnam Inc., 375 Hudson Street, New York, New York 10014, U.S.A.
Penguin Books Ltd, 80 Strand, London WC2R ORL England
Penguin Books Australia Ltd, Ringwood, Victoria, Australia
Penguin Books Canada Ltd, 10 Alcorn Avenue, Toronto, Ontario, Canada M4V 3B2
Penguin Books (N.Z.) Ltd, 182–190 Wairau Road, Auckland 10, New Zealand

Penguin Books Ltd, Registered Offices: Harmondsworth, Middlesex, England

First published by Plume, a member of Penguin Putnam Inc.

First Printing, January 2002
10 9 8 7 6 5 4 3 2

Copyright © Jason Kelly, 2002
All rights reserved.

Coca-Cola® is a registered trademark of the Coca-Cola Company, Inc.

We gratefully acknowledge the following

Permission to reprint an excerpt from "You Ought to Be Rich," from *Ladies' Home Journal* (August 1929), © Copyright 1929, Meredith Corporation. All rights reserved. Used with permission of *Ladies' Home Journal*.

Elliot Wave Theory used by permission of Equis International, makers of MetaStock.

Permission to reprint an excerpt from an article about Robert Sanborn, former manager of Oakmark mutual fund, in TheStreet.com (March 21 2000), © 2001 TheStreet.com, Inc. All rights reserved. Reprint permission granted by TheStreet.com (www.thestreet.com).

All quotations of Warren Buffett are copyrighted and are reprinted with the permission of Warren E. Buffett.

Ⓟ REGISTERED TRADEMARK—MARCA REGISTRADA

CIP data is available.
ISBN 0-452-28284-5

Printed in the United States of America
Set in Times New Roman

Without limiting the rights under copyright reserved above, no part of this publication may be reproduced, stored in or introduced into a retrieval system, or transmitted, in any form, or by any means (electronic, mechanical, photocopying, recording, or otherwise), without the prior written permission of both the copyright owner and the above publisher of this book.

BOOKS ARE AVAILABLE AT QUANTITY DISCOUNTS WHEN USED TO PROMOTE PRODUCTS OR SERVICES. FOR INFORMATION PLEASE WRITE TO PREMIUM MARKETING DIVISION, PENGUIN PUTNAM INC., 375 HUDSON STREET, NEW YORK, NEW YORK 10014.

Ten Steps to Do-It-Yourself Investing

1	Find $500 per Month to Invest	120
2	Think Like an Investor	57
3	Absorb Every Piece of Investment Information	59
4	Learn What Information to Ignore	67
5	Understand the Opportunity and Risk in Stocks	8
6	Understand That Many Non-stock Investments Are Riskier Than Stocks	28
7	Accept Stock Market Volatility	39
8	Manage Your Investments Online	92
9	Strongly Consider "The Simplest Investment Plan Ever"	116
10	Keep Investing Every Month for the Long Term	105

ACKNOWLEDGMENTS

With this *Neatest Little Guide*, the series has snuggled under the wing of a new editor, Gary Brozek. His suggestions created a careful blend of new material, to help returning readers become better investors, and recaps of old material, to help new readers get up to speed. I think you'll agree that the end result is worthy of the *Neatest Little Guide* moniker.

Doris Michaels remains the only agent I've ever had. There have been ups and downs and all arounds, but she's still the one.

A hearty thanks to the do-it-yourself investors who volunteered their time and financial information to me so that you could benefit from their mistakes and triumphs. Particularly helpful were Ron Moesle, Dick Sherman, Spike Dolomite, and Sharlene Choy.

Some of the world's finest investors and commentators allowed me to reprint their work. Thanks especially to Alan Abelson, Warren Buffett, and Peter Lynch.

Finally, to you, dear reader. You'll notice on the cover of this book that the word "bestselling" was used for the first time to describe the series. Thank you for making that happen. It's been a dream of mine for many years.

CONTENTS

Preface: Writing Through the Tornado — 1

1. The Glamour — 3

2. Opportunity and Risk in Stocks — 8

Make $9.2 Million by Accident — 8
   Such Were the Hardships — 10
   $15 to $250 in Five Months — 11
   Down Trends Among the Up — 13
   The 2000–2001 Bear Market — 15
   Constant Opportunity and Constant Risk — 18

The Winning System — 18
   Crafty Mr. Cook — 19
   Elliott's House of Mirrors — 23

Stock Market Dot Con — 25
   Pump-and-Dump — 25
   The Tale of Tokyo Joe — 26

The Risks You'll Happily Avoid — 28
   Real Estate Headaches — 29
   Limited Profit Partnerships — 30
   Becoming a Losing Lender — 32
   Getting Flimflammed — 33

Prime Bank Securities	34
New Utopia	34
Pyramid Schemes	35
Do-It-Yourself Investor Tools	**36**
Chapter Recap	36
Resources from This Chapter	*38*

3. The Calm Investor — 39

The Rafter and the Dow	**39**
Nobody Knows Where the Market Goes	40
Three Sure Things of Forecasting	42
You're Not the Market	43
Choose the Type of Risk That's Right for You	44
Risky, Greedy, and Fearful	**44**
Behavioral Finance	45
You'd Rather Get Ahead Than Be Ahead	46
Your Fluctuating Fortune	**49**
Don't Miss the Little Bursts	50
The Intelligent Risk Manager's Motto	50
Three Days per Year	51
Your Amorphous Money Glob	51
Do-It-Yourself Investor Tools	**52**
Chapter Recap	53
Resources from This Chapter	*54*

4. In the Oysters and Under The Rocks — 56

Think Like an Investor	**57**
Investment Info Everywhere	**59**
The Everywhere Info Is Just Fine, Thanks	**60**
The Sugar Water Bulletin	61
The Headlines of Akamai	63
What Shall We Read?	64
Learn What to Ignore	**67**
Avoiding Risky Behaviors	68

Don't Know and Don't Want to Know	69
The Siren Song of Investment Software	**71**
Dashed on The Rocks of Daytrading	71
The Saving Grace of a Database	74
Copy Successful Professionals	**76**
Do-It-Yourself Investor Tools	**78**
Chapter Recap	78
Resources from This Chapter	**80**

5. The Path to the Simplest Investment Plan Ever — 89

Brother-in-Law Brokers	**89**
Ever Hear of a Company Called Intel?	90
How to Save $792 per Order	92
The Art of the Order	**95**
A Stressful Argument About Stress Reduction	96
What a Morning	97
An Art of Your Own	98
Win Few, Win Big	**99**
Accidentally Owning the Market	100
The Safety of Twelve	102
The Idiotic Frontier	103
"If at First You Do Succeed, Quit Trying"	104
Keep Investing—The Advantage of Dollar–Cost Averaging	**105**
A Spoonful of Merck Every Month	106
Raskob Revisited	107
Wade In, Don't Dive	**108**
Alan's April Massacre	108
Either You Have Lost or You Will Lose	110
Pay Small Amounts to Learn	112
Stalking the Proper Excuses	114
The Simplest Investment Plan Ever	**116**
Do-It-Yourself Investor Tools	**116**
Chapter Recap	117
Resources from This Chapter	*118*

6. Finding $500 per Month — 120

Trim the Fat and Send It In — 121
- Renting from Ron, Buying from Dick — 121
- The $45,894 Honda — 123
- Food on the Floor — 125
- Suite Long-Distance Rates — 127
- The 40-Year Sofa Purchase Plan — 128
- Low Odds, Low Premiums — 129

Let the Good Times Pay — 132
- Paddling for Profit — 132
- Five-Star Cash — 133
- Getting Paid to Sleep — 133

Become a Baron, Magnate, or Tycoon — 134
- Child Fun and Mommy Money — 135
- Dollops of Paint and the Color of Cash — 137
- A Better Break Than Getting Elected to Congress — 138

Do-It-Yourself Investor Tools — 139
- Chapter Recap — 139

Resources from This Chapter — 141

7. And You're Off! — 143

Appendix 1: The View from My Piece of Flotsam — 146
- Dateline: June 27, 2001 — 146
- Kelly's Heroes: Stocking Up Your Recovery Portfolio — 148
- Good for All Eons — 151
- Kevlar 500/400 Portfolio — 154

Appendix 2: Your Risk Rundown — 156

Appendix 3: Fill Your 401(k) — 159

Appendix 4: Why I Detest Analysts — 162

Appendix 5: Do-It-Yourself Investor Tools — 165

This Book as a Brochure — 165

Resources from This Book — 169

Dedicated to the Victims of
September 11, 2001

Many of the people killed in the terrorist
attack on the United States worked in
finance. When they died, the markets closed
and nobody cared about investing. The markets
reopened six days later with the traditional bell,
heard that Monday against the roar of applause.
I clapped from my home in Los Angeles,
and I bought shares.

The markets will continue rising over time
as they have always done. Those whose time
horizon ended on that awful Tuesday
are not here to see it.

I wish they were.

The Neatest Little Guide to Do-It-Yourself Investing

PREFACE

Writing Through the Tornado

There's nothing I like more than a swirling tornado when I'm trying to write. And that's exactly what touched down on the stock market while this book came together. Prior to this book, my *Neatest Little Guides* were written during the runaway bull market of the 1990s. This one started there in summer 1999 and ended in early summer 2001 during the worst bear market in Nasdaq history. In 1999 the Nasdaq gained 86 percent. From March 10, 2000 to April 4, 2001, it lost 68 percent. Yes, these pages straddle the best and worst that the stock market has to offer.

Frankly, the reversal in the market worked wonders for my belief in do-it-yourself investing. Why? Because the experts led everybody astray. In February 2000, analysts gave 72 percent of stocks they evaluated ratings of "strong buy" or "buy." In December 2000, still 72 percent. In June 2001, a hearty 67 percent. In February 2000, only 0.7 percent of analyst stock ratings were "underperform" or "sell." Their warnings increased to 1.2 percent in June 2001, as I write these words to you (and guess that we're nearing the bottom). The analysts, dear reader, are morons.

You are your own best money manager because money isn't hard to manage. The media is. Emotions are. Claims of a new economy are. But buying good investments at good prices isn't. Self-management kept risk low in 1999 and, lo and behold, kept it down in 2001. Careful investing will keep working no matter what the market does.

For best results, do it yourself.

1 / The Glamour

Ah, the life of the independent investor. Every time you hear those words you envision private jets and weekend conferences at resort islands. You hear blenders spinning out frothy tropical drinks. You see languid faces and pristine Italian suits and of course you catch the sound of that musical word whispered into cell phones from the side of a lounge: *buy*.

At least that's what you would have seen and heard in January 2000. But by January 2001 you saw the bubbles burst. The drinks kept pouring, though. You can count on that in good times and bad.

Let's go back in time. It's January 2000 and things have never looked better for the USA. Profits are up, the market is up, wages are up, unemployment is down, and the fear that Y2K would wipe out computers and ravage the economy has proved false. You're feeling good. Not just good, but *good!* You got your biggest-ever year-end bonus, and you are not going to miss the opportunity to get rich in the stock market. Not this time.

In 1995 you put your bonus in a balanced mutual fund after watching the Nasdaq slide 3 percent in 1994. In 1995 it rose 40 percent and you missed it. By then it was too late to catch the profits, so you put your 1995 bonus into the same balanced mutual fund and sat on the sidelines in 1996 when the Nasdaq rose another 23 percent.

You were seething. But you kept thinking it had to slide back now. It just had to. The experts thought so; your uncle thought so. Only the jerk three offices down the hall thought it would go up forever because he had invested everything in technology stocks and was driving a new sport utility vehicle that he could easily park on top of your commuter car. His license plate read STOCK UP. You couldn't wait for the inevitable market slide to shut him up. Surely 1997 would be the year.

So you put your bonus into a money market mutual fund, even safer than the balanced fund. You'd have wads of cash ready to buy the jerk's deflated stocks for a fraction of their current prices. Then the Nasdaq rose 22 percent in 1997 and your coworker bought a time share on Maui.

Come on, 1998! sink this son of a gun—this can't go on forever. You add your bonus to the money market fund and the Nasdaq gains 40 percent in 1998. You've earned enough in interest to buy a new suit. Your tech-stock-slinging coworker moved into a bigger house and now has a Corvette the same color as his sport utility vehicle. Its license plate reads STOCK ON. You have never hated anybody more than you hate him.

But 1999 will grind him to a nub for sure. You've missed so many profits for so long that getting in now would be preposterous. Nothing rises indefinitely. So you remain in cash while the Nasdaq rises 86 percent in 1999, the same amount as your blood pressure.

Eighty-six percent, for crying out loud! That's it. If you can't beat 'em, join 'em. You take your fat 1999 bonus and sit at the table in January 2000 and buy the tech-est of the tech stocks to make up for lost time. You buy Amazon.com at $64, CMGI at $130, Internet Capital Group at $134, JDS Uniphase at $186, and Yahoo at $354. The remainder of your money you plow into top tech funds Kinetics Internet and PBHG Technology & Communication. In 1999, they returned 216 percent and 244 percent respectively. Now you are loaded and can't wait to show that pipsqueak down the hall.

The Nasdaq drops 39 percent in 2000. Kinetics Internet plummets 51 percent and PBHG Tech falls 41 percent. Amazon.com closes the year at $16, CMGI at $6, Internet Capital Group at $3, JDS Uniphase at $42, and Yahoo at $30. And your commuter car needs a new radiator. Ah, the life of an independent investor. Ain't it glamorous?

Maybe you didn't get hit quite so squarely between the eyes. A lot of people who lost money in 2000 were just giving back some of the obscene profits from the previous five years, like the jerk down the hall. But somebody played the unhappy part in that scenario and it just might have been you. Thank goodness it's all behind us now, right? We can wipe the back of our hands across our foreheads and just be happy that *this* year's bonus won't have to take the same rappeling trip. Things are safer on this side of the chasm.

Wrong. The stock market always behaves this way. It always has and always will, as you'll read in more detail later. For now, just know that before 2000 there was 1990 when the Nasdaq lost 18 percent and October 19, 1987, when the market dropped 23 percent in a single day. Or how about the 1970s as a decade? The Dow didn't stay above its 1969 high until 1982. Those were fun times. Pity Xerox investors. Shares in that company ended 2000 below their 1972 price.

Yet some people make money at it. They know that investing involves risk, but they make it a prudent risk. They manage the risk so it returns more profits than losses. And they're not necessarily doing it with expensive advisors at a resort island—they might be doing it themselves from home like my grandfather.

As a boy, I loved visiting him in Arcadia, California. One night, he disappeared into his home office and closed the door behind him. I asked my grandmother what he was doing in there. "Oh," she said, "probably making millions." Curious, I tiptoed outside onto the lawn, listening to crickets and the garden fountain as I made my way to the top of a small embankment. Through the window I watched Grandpa at his desk, arranging magazines, underlining sentences, and taking notes in pencil. Without a day of formal investment training in his life and using only common resources, he spent one evening per month in that office to make a stock market fortune. You can do the same as a do-it-yourself investor.

Don't believe me? Evan Tolvin was a graduate student at the University of Colorado in 1992. I met him there during my dismal effort to learn computer programming. He attempted to show me the digital ropes over cups of coffee in Boulder.

One evening, he sat back from our book-covered table in the newest coffee shop in town, both hands cuddling a warm mug, and looked around the place. It was new and few people had heard of it. "Starbucks," he said. "What a strange name. Sure is good coffee, though, and look how many people are in line. I wonder if they're public?" A "public" company offers its stock so that anybody can invest. Starbucks was public, and in 1993 Evan bought a thousand shares for a split-adjusted $5 each. After that he never wanted to have coffee anywhere else. As of January 2001, his Starbucks holding was worth $49,000 and actually gained during Terrible 2000. Evan never met with a broker. He never sought financial counseling. He just paid attention to life and did it himself.

If my grandfather were alive today, he would marvel at the investment resources available. He had a handful of business magazines to read, we have dozens. He had one daily business newspaper to read, we have three. He listened to an occasional radio program with top business news, we have twenty-four hours of constant investment talk on radio and television. And the Internet? He never heard of it, never imagined it, and would have trouble grasping how much information it puts in front of us.

Today, you have access to investment tools every bit as powerful as those used by professionals. In many cases they're the same tools used by professionals. But you want to know something? Access to the same tools isn't all it takes to succeed. We've had access to the same tools used by master chefs, carpenters, and tailors for years. That doesn't mean we can cook a five-star meal, build show-quality kitchen cabinetry, or sew a world-class tuxedo. Skill and training must accompany those mixing bowls, those hammers and rasps, those needles and pinking shears.

The tools are the easy part, the skills and training, the hard—but not the impossible—part. A do-it-yourself investor can make money in the market, and I've found patterns among the most successful investors I know. Revealing those patterns is the purpose of this book. No home office, regardless of its cornucopia of websites, books, magazines, newsletters, charting software, beepers, television investment programs, and radio talk shows can rescue the poorly prepared investor. No adequately prepared investor will be stopped by a lack of resources. But unite the well-stocked office with the prepared investor and you've got a winner.

You'll find tools and techniques within each chapter that follows. To make it easy to find those resources for yourself, I list them in a toolbox like the one below and end each chapter with a section called "Do-It-Yourself Investor Tools" that summarizes the main points and lists the tools you'll want to try when managing your own investments. I take that one step further by collecting the tools from all the chapters in Appendix 5.

> **Tools are highlighted in a box like this and listed at the end of each chapter and in Appendix 5.**

Being an independent investor might not always be as glamorous as portrayed in movies. But it can be a lot of fun and profitable too.

Now let's go make you some money.

2 / Opportunity and Risk in Stocks

The stock market goes through overall trends, either up or down, or sometimes sideways. During every trend, however, constant opportunity and constant risk present themselves. We tend to forget that and focus instead on the trend of the moment. In the 1990s bull market, the name of the show was "All Profits, All the Time!" In the bear market of 2000–2001, it became "What Goes Up Must Come Down."

The constant opportunity and constant risk make the stock market your best bet for getting ahead—if you know how to manage risk and know how to manage yourself. In this chapter we'll have a closer look at opportunity and risk in the market, pick apart the myth of the Winning System, steer clear of stock fraud, and revel in avoiding some inferior investments that *won't* be eating up your money.

Make $9.2 Million by Accident

Most of today's do-it-yourself investors began in the 1990s, one of the best decades in market history. How good was it? It's hard to know where to begin, but Cisco's not a bad story.

Say you had nothing to do on February 16, 1990, when Cisco Systems went public at $18. What the heck, you think, this company makes something related to computers, so it probably has a mildly promising future. You sell the extra car in the garage, put $9,000 into the magical CSCO, and never tell anybody. You buy 500 shares.

Five years later you glance at your brokerage statement and notice that you now own 8,000 shares, thanks to four 2–1 splits.

> **Stock split:** when a company increases the number of shares you own without increasing your equity. That means your account value is the same immediately after the split because you have more shares at a lower price. For instance, a 2-1 stock split would turn 500 shares at $18 into 1,000 shares at $9, a value of $9,000 either way. Companies split their stock to make the price affordable to more people. Splitting usually signals that a company is optimistic about its future.

Then another number catches your eye and you can scarcely believe it. There must be a typo in that market value column. NOTE TO SELF, you scribble on the outside of the envelope. CALL BROKER AND TELL HIM STATEMENT IS WRONG. A few weeks go by and you get wrapped up in spring vacation, then it's summer, and before you know it you've forgotten to ever reprimand the broker about your mistyped statement.

Five years later—your life is very hectic—you glance at the latest statement from your broker and notice that you now have 72,000 shares after a 2–1 split, two 3–2 splits, and another 2–1. While your broker missed a minor typo on the 1995 statement, he has let the value of a third-world gross national product escape detection on the 2000 statement. Or could that number be right? The market value column for CSCO shows that your $9000 investment has turned into $9,216,000.

Come again? You whip out your pocket calculator and run 72,000 shares times a February 2000 price of $128 and get, sure enough, $9.2 million. "Honey," you shout to the other room, "did I ever mention that I bought a stock back in 1990?"

Such Were the Hardships

Cisco was quite a performer, but it wasn't alone. Other companies would have made your fortune in less time.

"The best thing I ever bought was on a lark," reports Bruce Featherstone of Downer's Grove, Illinois, meaning CMGI, an Internet holding company. He teaches mathematics to high schoolers, so he has a firm grasp on what it means when an investment does well.

If you're familiar with the course of Internet stocks in the last half of the 1990s, then you know the name CMGI. It develops Internet companies and runs a venture fund focused on the Internet, which makes owning stock in CMGI like owning an Internet mutual fund. The stock began its public life on January 25, 1994, at a price of $8, although split-adjusted it was just 17 cents. When I spoke with Bruce in January 2000, the stock was trading at a price of $130. Now there's a story for the kids. $10,000 in CMGI would have become $7.6 million in six years.

But if you can believe this, as Bruce is about to tell you, the CMGI story got even better. "As an owner of CMGI shares, I received a letter offering me the chance to buy IPO shares of a company CMGI owned called NaviSite. I read the profile of NaviSite and saw that it outsourced web operations for other companies, a field that CMGI projected would grow tremendously. I saw the offer as a good chance to buy at $12 or $14 and then sell on the first day of trading at $40 or $50 a share, after the usual runup."

He bought at $14 in October 1999. As predicted the stock ran up past $50 a share then began settling back. "I watched profits evaporating before my eyes and my investor friends were saying, 'Take the profit! Take the profit!' So I placed a stop order at $28 as the price descended through the 30s. It came within a few bucks of hitting that stop, but never quite touched it."

Stop order: an order placed with your broker to sell a stock at a specified price below its current price. The order stays on the books for a day or until cancelled, depending on your instructions. If NaviSite shares had reached $28, the broker would have sold Bruce's shares.

So he held onto his full portfolio of shares. "Now here we are in March 2000, and the thing is at $330 a share. Can you believe it? That's more than a 23-bagger. I'm kicking myself for not investing even more."

Such were the hardships of U.S. investors in the 1990s and first two months of 2000. There were times when we could have made more but, darn it, we didn't. Bruce's $1400 invested in the NaviSite IPO became $33,000 in five months. He was allowed only 100 shares at the IPO but he could have bought more at $30 when the price settled to that price. Let's say he invested another $8,600 at $30 to make his principal investment an even $10,000. He would have owned 387 shares, which in March would have been worth $127,710.

What kind of schlepp turns $1,400 into $33,000 when he could have turned $10,000 into $128,000? Clearly, a spineless amateur. Those were times for fast trigger fingers and red-blooded commitment, not waffling with a $28 stop order. Anybody worth their salt in the raging American bull market had no day job. Bruce, you'll note, was still teaching high school. (Stop giggling in the back.)

$15 to $250 in Five Months

For a much better story of money management and not one of squandered opportunity, we go now to Cynthia Braus in Green River, Wyoming. She is a lab worker at a blood bank and remembers well the days she spent studying biology at the University of Colorado. There in the labs of Nobel Prize winner Thomas Czech, she looked through microscopes and shook vials of fluid. She believes we will one day cure cancer, and she wants to own the company that does so. "Let me know when you find it," I told her.

"In summer 1999, I found one that I thought might help," she said. "It's called Celera Genomics. It helps pharmaceutical companies analyze genetic information. I liked what [CEO] Craig Venter said in news stories. When I read that some biotech mutual funds were buying shares, I decided to invest along with them. I bought at different times over the summer and fall at an average price of $15 per share, split adjusted. I ended up with 1200 shares."

Total investment: $18,000.
Price of a fifteen-dollar share as of February 2000: $250.

Gain in five months: 1,567 percent.
New market value of initial investment: $300,000.
Status of this desirable woman: single.*

The 1990s and early 2000 made lots of people wealthy in short periods of time. New investors arrived daily as the stock market became the moneymaker of choice.

Microsoft, considered by many to be the kingpin of tech stocks, began 1990 with a split-adjusted price of $1.23 and ended 1999 with a price just shy of $117. That's a ten-year run of 9,412 percent. A $10,000 investment became $951,000, and at the end of the decade, Microsoft was the biggest company in the world.

From 1997 to 2000 CMGI stock gained 14,000 percent, Yahoo 7,500 percent, JDS Uniphase 6,000 percent, and eBay 3,000 percent. A mere hundred bucks of stock in EMC back in 1988 was worth $53,000 twelve years later. In the two years following its 1998 initial public offering, Broadcom went from a split-adjusted $6 per share to more than $200. Eat your hearts out, state lotteries.

Versions of the Investor's English dictionary printed in the United States in early 2000 are missing words like *hardship*, *struggle*, *enduring*, and *sacrifice*. Those words were not used much and were increasingly seen as being antiquated, better left to history books and occasional stories from people who remembered fireside chats. In place of the omitted words you'll find terms printed in bold such as *genomic*, *asynchronous*, *dot com*, and *margin*. Such vocabulary was useful in everyday conversation with folks on buses and at the mall who may have looked at you quizzically when confronted with an anachronism like *hardship*.

Yet the stock market has returned about 11 percent a year since 1926. That figure used to be cited as an accomplishment but looks like chump change compared to the 1990s. Why, you may ask, is that long-term figure so low? Because the market isn't always in 1990s bull mode. An invisible weight holds down the benefit of high-flying times. That invisible weight is *risk*—comprised of market declines, individual company troubles, political shenanigans, and the occasional wayward comet. We forget about the invisible weight when gaining 9,412 percent in ten years, but it doesn't forget about

---

*Eligible bachelors may visit my website for her phone number.

us. It's always present, a shadow among the lit, and when you factor the down trends into the up trends you get an overall long-term average of just 11 percent per year.

It's time to look at the invisible, shadowy, risky side of the stock market.

Down Trends Among the Up

Once I convey how phenomenal the 1990s were, it's no difficult matter to get you nodding about investing in the stock market. It's likely that you now have your paycheck close at hand, waiting to be put to use to help turn a quick profit. Surely, though, you realize that it's not all roses even in high-flying times. Penny stocks still go from being great buys to being worth nothing. Top companies still hit the skids here and there. Individual investors make the wrong allocations. Ever-present risk always casts its shadow on somebody.

It chose the Oakmark mutual fund in the late 1990s. The fund performed well in the early 1990s under the guidance of value investor extraordinaire, Robert Sanborn. A value investor looks for bargain stocks, shares that are cheap when compared to the long-term prospects of the company. By contrast, growth investors, the champions of the 1990s, are willing to pay higher prices for companies that are growing sales and profits quickly. In 1993, Sanborn posted a 31 percent gain, beating the S&P 500 by more than 20 percent and besting 98 percent of his peers. That did it for a lot of onlookers. Their money was in.

> **S&P 500:** The Standard & Poor's 500 is a stock index like the Dow Jones Industrial Average and the Nasdaq Composite. It tracks 500 leading companies and accounts for 80 percent of the New York Stock Exchange. It's considered a measure of older established companies while the Nasdaq measures newcomers.

Lo and behold, the headlines on March 21, 2000, announced that Sanborn was relinquishing control of the fund to a peer. *TheStreet.com* had this to say:

Sanborn's strict approach has put him at the bottom of the value category's scrap heap. Despite tech stocks' sharp run-up, he stuck to his guns and avoided them and other pricey sectors. Instead he focused even more heavily on cheaper Old Economy stocks, such as Philip Morris and top holding Brunswick, down 27.6 percent and 11.3 percent, respectively, so far this year. On February 29, the fund's average price-to-earnings ratio was 14.7, less than half the S&P 500's. The fund's commitment to deep value in a growth market shows in its returns. Sanborn trails 99 percent or 100 percent of his peers over the past one-, three-, five- and ten-year periods, according to Morningstar. Since January 1, the fund is down more than 15 percent, trailing nearly all of its peers and the S&P 500 by more than 14 percentage points.

Sanborn can hardly be faulted for a market that relegated value investing to the scrap heap. His approach to investing worked wonders before, and he knew it would one day work wonders again. But not in 1999 when—*yippee!*—NaviSite was going public and you too could own a piece of the action. Philip Morris? Give us a break. Don't they make cigarettes or something? If they were selling those cigs globally at brownlung.com, *then* we might have been interested.

Like so many of us, Sanborn threw in the towel just as the fight was about to turn. Philip Morris doubled in 2000 and the Oakmark Fund gained 12 percent while the Nasdaq drank Drano and fell 39 percent. Sanborn had good company while underperforming the runaway market. None other than the great Warren Buffett, he of 24-percent average annual gains for the past 35 years as chairman of Berkshire Hathaway, eked out a puny 0.5 percent gain in 1999. That was 20.5 percent worse than the S&P 500.

In his own words, "We had the worst absolute performance of my tenure and, compared to the S&P, the worst relative performance as well." This at a time when high school math teachers gained 23 times their money in five months. A time when lab technicians turned $18,000 into $300,000.

What went wrong? Buffett deliberately avoided technology. He wrote in Berkshire's 1999 annual report:

> We believe these companies [in which we invest] have important competitive advantages that will endure over time. This attribute, which makes for good long-term investment results, is one Charlie and I occasionally believe we can identify. More often, however, we can't—not, at least, with a high degree of conviction. This explains, by the way, why we don't own stocks of tech companies, even though we share the general view that our society will be transformed by their products and services. Our problem—which we can't solve by studying up—is that we have no insights into which participants in the tech field possess a truly *durable* competitive advantage.

He went on to warn against a steep drop in the market:

> If investor expectations become more realistic—and they almost certainly will—the market adjustment is apt to be severe, particularly in sectors in which speculation has been concentrated. Berkshire will someday have opportunities to deploy major amounts of cash in equity markets—we are confident of that. But, as the song goes, "Who knows where or when?" Meanwhile, if anyone starts explaining to you what is going on in the truly manic portions of this "enchanted" market, you might remember still another line of song: "Fools give you reasons, wise men never try."

I wish somebody would have kept that guy away from the punch bowl. Everything was swimmingly fun until he arrived and started talking market adjustments. Then we needed to get out those old dictionaries still in print with the words *hardship* and *sacrifice* and brace ourselves for a crash of epic proportions, with much gnashing of teeth and rending of clothes.

The 2000-2001 Bear Market

And it came. Boy, did it ever. The year 2000 began on an optimistic note. After 1999's bangup performance (Nasdaq up 86 percent, Dow up 27 percent) investors on the sidelines were tired of missing the party. Who cares that the Fed raised interest rates three times in 1999 and warned of a slowing economy? *Everybody into the pool.*

It was warm and fun with umbrella drinks all around for the first two months. The Nasdaq gained 19 percent in February alone. But the Fed kept raising rates. On March 10, the Nasdaq peaked at 5,133 and ended the day at 5,049. In the first two weeks of April it lost 27 percent. It ended 2000 at 2,471, a 39 percent loss for the year and a 51 percent loss from the March 10 close. The year 2000 was the worst in Nasdaq history as of our publication date of January 2002. It wasn't much fun for the other indexes either. The S&P 500 lost 10 percent and the Dow lost 6 percent. Things didn't just magically improve in 2001, either. By the end of March, the Nasdaq was down an additional 26 percent. On April 4, 2001, it closed at 1,639, a loss of 68 percent from the March 10, 2000, close.

An accountant friend told me about one of his clients who watched the April 2000 stock slide and took out a second mortgage on his house to buy cheap shares. Stocks kept sliding. He took out a third on his home in August to buy more shares. Stocks slid again. He opened a home-equity line of credit in October and bought more shares. In November, the Nasdaq lost 23 percent and in December the bank foreclosed on the man's home.

Pets.com ran a popular ad campaign featuring a sock puppet singing the Blood, Sweat & Tears song, "What goes up must come down." I wonder if the little guy knew he prophesied the death of his own company? Pets.com didn't just come down in price during 2000, it went out of business. Joining it were Toysmart.com, iCast, Eve.com, and other gems of what was once called the "New Economy." Not yet defunct but on the verge of joining this group by year's end were a host of former stars. Here's the rogues gallery:

Stock	12/29/2000 Close	Off 52-Week High
PlanetRx.com	$0.28	−99.8%
eToys	$0.19	−99.4%
E-Stamp	$0.19	−99.3%
Engage	$0.75	−99.2%
Neoforma	$0.81	−99.0%

Stock	12/29/2000 Close	Off 52-Week High
drkoop.com	$0.22	−98.7%
NaviSite	$2.34	−98.6%
Drugstore.com	$0.91	−97.7%
EMusic.com	$0.28	−97.7%
Webvan	$0.47	−97.5%
CMGI	$5.59	−96.6%
Akamai	$21.06	−93.9%
Peapod	$0.78	−93.2%
Inktomi	$17.88	−92.6%
MP3.com	$3.63	−91.0%

It was the kind of year that Alan Abelson, the curmudgeonly columnist at *Barron's*, dreams of. His specialty is making fun of people who lose money, and I write that with every drop of bitterness my pores can ooze because I'm occasionally one of those people. On January 1, 2001, Alan's column contained this summary of the prior year:

> We're in a whole new world, so get used to it. A world in which the bloom is off the boom, technology has lost its edge, and we're witness to the most horrible spectacle since the Rape of the Sabine Women—the Sack of the Nasdaq.

A great many horrible spectacles have occurred since the Sabine tribe attended the games in Rome and a good percentage of them trump the falling Nasdaq, but Alan is generally correct in his assessment. The year 2000 was one hell of a crummy ride for most investors, and it kept getting crummier in 2001.

Yet somebody owned Philip Morris, which doubled in 2000; somebody invested in the Schroder Micro Cap fund, which gained 148 percent; and somebody held onto Green Mountain Coffee, which saw its stock go from $8 on January 3, 2000, to $50 on December 29, 2000. On January 12, 2001, Green Mountain Coffee split 2–1 and its stock rose an additional 36 percent by June 1.

Constant Opportunity and Constant Risk

The market is a land of constant opportunity and constant risk. Don't expect things to change because your money has finally arrived. And don't expect things to change because somebody says we've entered a "new economy." It might be a new economy, but it's the same collection of opportunities and perils that we've always seen. New economy, old story.

Even during heady times like the 1990s and early 2000, the market threw both knives and creampuffs. During troubled times, some people do just fine. They don't take too much risk; they don't take too little. They take just the right amount to get ahead over time without getting financially sacked on the way. The stock market is a down and dirty, rough and tumble place to put your money. It has always been that way and will continue that way forever. There are winners and losers no matter which way the general indexes are headed.

Through it all, stocks remain the best place for your money. Suddenly those historic 11-percent annual returns don't seem so bad. Forget the Microsofts and CMGIs and NaviSites for a moment. Forget the Philip Morrises and Green Mountain Coffees. They're trees in the forest getting different amounts of light as clouds we don't control move across the sky. One thing we can see from afar is that the forest itself always has light somewhere and as a whole has grown fat and bushy through the years.

The Winning System

The greatest peril you may ever face is not the turbulence of the market but the shysters who claim to have it all figured out. It goes something like this: You're situated in your office having just read about the volatility of markets. You're convinced that the worst is behind us and that now is a super buying opportunity, and besides, didn't I just say that somebody is always winning? It's finally your turn to make some money, and there beside you is a glossy mailer from Wade Cook Financial Corporation. It says Mr. Cook went from driving a cab to making more than $10,000 a day in the stock market. He'll teach you his strategies at an upcoming seminar. "What timing!" you say.

Welcome to Wall Street's oldest myth, the myth of The Winning System.

Crafty Mr. Cook

You continue reading the brochure. It says the stock market can be used like a money machine to improve your cash flow. Sounds good. Mr. Cook has developed a foolproof system that uses options and trading on margin. He claims he can double his money every 2½ to 4 months. Heh, heh. Wait until your brother-in-law sees the riches piling up in your coffers. You see a dance floor and a full orchestra playing beneath a ribbon with your name on it and something about being a benefactor. You should be seeing a red flag. Let's run Wade Cook's numbers.

We'll be conservative and go with the 4-month doubling period. If you start Cook's "money machine" system with $1,000 in January, you will have $2,000 at the end of April. You reinvest that $2000 at the beginning of May and end up with $4,000 at the end of August. The $4,000 is reinvested at the beginning of September to end your money machine year with a tidy $8,000. Your gain for the first year was 700 percent. With only $7000 profit, however, you're still working a day job.

Ever faithful, you begin year two. The $8000 becomes $16,000 in the first four months, which becomes $32,000 in the second, which becomes $64,000 by the end of the year. Another 700 percent annual return, but this time with a $56,000 profit. Things are looking up. Year three turns the reinvested $64,000 into $128,000 in the first four months, which becomes $256,000 in the second, which becomes $512,000 by the end of the year. You yawn as you tally up the 700 percent return for a profit of $448,000.

At this rate not only have you quit your day job, but by the end of your ten-year run of annual 700 percent returns you are a trillionaire. You write a thank-you note to Wade Cook for his nifty system and then tender an offer for Microsoft.

You would think that such a gangbuster claim as doubling your money every 2½ to 4 months would have you and most others laughing on the floor. Instead, it has a lot of people closing their eyes to champagne wishes and caviar dreams—and attending a free seminar for more information. I met a person at an investment conference in Las Vegas who had attended a free Wade Cook seminar and told me about it.

"It was at a hotel, with around sixty other people. Wade Cook himself wasn't there, so another fellow who worked for him ran the show. He told us the paid seminar was very expensive and only intended for people who are serious about achieving the American dream. Wade would be there for that one."

But what did the free seminar teach? "Not much. It was basically a commercial for the real seminar. The lecturer told us to forget about annual rates of return because they're boring. He said it's much better to concentrate on monthly or weekly returns. Buy and hold stopped working when the new economy kicked into action."

(I immediately faxed this breakthrough to Warren Buffett's office in Omaha. I also took the extra step of writing on the fax that he can stop obsessing over annual returns because they don't matter anymore. Only big monthly returns count. I believe my faxed tipsheet will help Mr. Buffett immensely.)

"The lecturer showed some charts on what can happen to money growing at 20 percent a month. The system achieves that performance with options and something called rolling stocks." A rolling stock is one that fluctuates in price between an upper and lower limit. The money machine system supposedly shows when the stock hits its lower limit and you should buy. Later it tells you when it hits its upper limit and you should sell. Repeating this cycle creates the money machine.

That was about it for the free infomercial. It was time to ante up for the millionaire training program. "The cost of the twelve-month millionaire apprenticeship was more than $20,000, but after the discounts it was available to us that day for only $6,000. The three-day seminar was $15,000 but available that day for $3,200. The lecturer explained that if we couldn't afford the price, then we really needed the classes."

That's one version of The Winning System, albeit an almost ridiculously avoidable one. Another person I spoke with actually paid money to attend the deluxe seminar and reported that half of the time was spent hawking products sold at the back of the room. There's definitely a "money machine" in action here, but it appears to take your money rather than provide you with more.

"There was a guarantee," my acquaintance remembered. "If within three months we weren't shown three stocks that made at least 300 percent, we'd get a full refund on the seminar. Our leader called it the 3-3-3 guarantee."

The guarantee defines the 300 percent as being annualized, an interesting gambit considering the seminar leader's disdain for annual returns. Annualizing the 300 percent return of the guarantee means a one-day, one-percent move qualifies. Anybody can find three stocks that go up at least one percent on at least one day of a three-month time period. You could find every one of them on the Dow. How much premium-priced research and analysis would that take?

> **Dow:** The Dow Jones Industrial Average is maintained by the editors of the *Wall Street Journal*. It consists of 30 of the largest companies in America, like Coca-Cola, Home Depot, and Microsoft. Everybody knows everything about such companies.

I did a little checking around on Wade Cook after first hearing about these seminars. I too wanted to achieve 20-percent monthly returns and ever since I was a kid I've wanted to be a trillionaire. At last I'd found my big chance. Come to find out, Wade runs a company called Wade Cook Financial Corporation that trades under the symbol WADE.OB. I found in its November 1999 10-Q statement a list of pending lawsuits including this gem:

> Stuart E. Mac Gregor, II vs. Wade B. Cook, Wade Cook Seminars, Inc., Information Quest, Inc. and Wade Cook Financial Corporation. On September 21st, 1999, Mr. Stuart Mac Gregor filed suit in the Superior Court of Washington for King County against Mr. Cook and the Company. The complaint alleges that Mr. Cook and the Company committed negligent misrepresentation, fraud, and conspiracy to commit fraud in selling products and services to Mr. Mac Gregor.*

---

*On February 28, 2001, the company was granted a protective order limiting the scope of Mr. Mac Gregor's discovery requests. Not surprisingly, the company denied that it has engaged in any unlawful practices.

Nah, come on. The promise of 700 percent annual returns is negligent misrepresentation? I thought this was The Winning System. Clearly, Mr. Mac Gregor simply missed one of Wade's important bulletins or called the wrong hotline. There must be some mistake.

Or maybe not. I read in the June 2000 issue of *Reader's Digest* that a businessman in Florida lost $13,000 in the money machine. The article goes on to reveal that even the creators of the money machine can't kick it into gear:

> Prospective students might be more skeptical of Cook's guidance if they knew that in 1997, while his company had more than $60 million in net revenues from its financial seminars, it actually *lost* $806,000 on trading securities. A spokesman for WCFC responds that the company made $837,000 trading stocks in 1998. In other words, it took two years of trading in a bull market for the company to just about break even in an area where it boasts expertise.

For all the trillionaire potential of Wade's money machine system, the stock market itself doesn't seem to find WADE.OB stock particularly valuable. It rose to more than $4 after going public in fall of 1997, then dove over the next three and a half years to a price of 15 cents. While the indefatigable money machine system claims to churn out 700-percent annual returns, WADE stock lost 96 percent or thereabouts—but who's really counting anymore?

It occurred to me that if the money machine worked so well, Wade wouldn't put such effort into selling books and apprenticeship programs and seminars. Far better, it seems to me, to kick back and enjoy those 700-percent annual returns. The explanation made itself clear to me in an article profiling the man. Turns out this isn't just about money. His "real passion is helping others improve their lives." Perhaps a more suitable moniker would be the "passionate money machine" system.

That was the end of my research on Wade Cook Financial Corporation. I had enough dirt under my nails to hang my head sadly, trillionaire dreams dashed yet again. You can safely throw away that promising brochure.

Elliott's House of Mirrors

But don't despair. Where one winning system falls short, there's always another. It's often presented as a complex numerical formula that will reveal the direction of the stock market to the select few who follow the system.

"Ever hear of the Elliott Wave?" Cellah Randall asked me between seminars at a San Francisco investment conference. I had, but kept quiet to listen to her version of this well-known system. Cellah, you see, is a statistician working for a major healthcare corporation in Illinois. She knows numbers, and whenever somebody who knows numbers turns on a faucet of facts about making money in the stock market, I'm a dry sponge.

"It's a system built on Dow theory and tied to cycles in nature. You know, the stock market moves in waves just like natural phenomena, and you can predict where it's heading by identifying the patterns."

"I see, and what are those patterns?" I asked in a low voice.

"The basic pattern is predicated on action following reaction." I wrote it down, nodding like a bobble-headed doll as she continued. "There are five waves in the main trend direction followed by three corrective waves in the other direction."

"So, five steps forward, three steps back?" I ventured.

"Right. This so-called 5–3 move completes an Elliott cycle."

"Then it starts over again?"

"Yes, but not always how you'd think and not always in the time frame you expect. Usually the 5–3 cycle becomes two subdivisions of a bigger 5–3 cycle."

There's a general rule about The Winning System that goes like this: The more complicated it is, the more difficult it is to test and therefore disprove. Buried deep within the website of Equis International, publisher of MetaStock software, is this summary:

> Elliott Wave Theory holds that each wave within a wave count contains a complete 5–3 wave count of a smaller cycle. The longest wave count is called the Grand Supercycle. Grand Supercycle waves are comprised of Supercycles, and Supercycles are comprised of Cycles. This process continues into Primary, Intermediate, Minute, Minuette, and Sub-minuette waves.

Scratch your head a second and ask yourself, Doesn't this sound expansive enough to explain *any* movement in the stock market? For that matter, doesn't it contain enough variables (within variables, mind you) to explain *any* pattern in the weather, holiday emotional stress, and even the growth of that mold in my refrigerator? Yes! This is a downright useful theory to know.

But I couldn't help noticing a glaring hole in my notes. "Where is the market heading next?" I asked.

"It's tough to say," replied Ms. Randall, my statistician advisor. "Accurate predictions depend entirely on accurate wave counts. Few people can agree on when the last wave ended and the new wave began. It's exceedingly subjective." I submit that your guess is as good as hers or mine or even Ralph Nelson Elliott's, after whom the theory is named. Which, unfortunately, removes all predictive value and therefore *all* value of the theory. Sure, somebody correctly picks the direction of the market occasionally and credits Elliott Wave Theory for the success, but then again some people call the market correctly using water sticks and sunspots. The market has to go somewhere.

"I correctly called the direction of the market once by just lying in bed," says Brian Dinneen of Blackfoot, Idaho. A carpet layer for twelve years, he invests everything in large company stocks like Hewlett-Packard, General Electric, and AT&T. "People at work were talking about how the market was going to fall. It's gotta give they said because it's gone up too far too fast. They were going to sell in the morning and advised me to do the same. I was ready to follow them when I thought to myself, *What if it doesn't?* I couldn't make up my mind, so I just lay in bed until the urge to sell passed; then I went to work. Nobody talked much about the market that day. On the way home, I heard on the radio that the Dow rose almost 2 percent."

It's obvious to me that we can explain Brian's approach simply as a sub-minuette wave of laziness within a larger cycle of confusion contained inside yet a larger supercycle of peer-group misinformation—easily within the reach of Elliott Wave Theory.

"I can never tell where the market is headed," Brian confessed. "I tried following systems for a time, but none of them worked reliably. I'm just betting that the market will generally work its way higher like it has forever. I know there'll be down times here and there, but overall I think it will rise. If it doesn't, then I guess I should have bought something else." Now there's The Winning System presented in a way that finally makes sense.

Stock Market Dot Con

Even if you're not taken by somebody's winning system, you might be snookered by stock market fraud. A cold wind blows against the windows of your warm home office. Some people are not playing nicely.

Pump-and-Dump

"The Internet has made suckers of a lot of people," says Gary Halford of Bay City, Michigan. "Everybody watched tech company stocks go crazy and then heard you could find out about them online. But they usually got stock market dot con. In discussion forums and offbeat research sites I see more pump-and-dump than solid information." Pump-and-dump is when a thinly traded stock that's usually held by a few people is touted across the Internet so that other investors learn of the great opportunity and pile in. That's the pump. The sudden demand drives the stock price higher, at which point the pumpers turn around and sell at the high price for a quick profit. That's the dump. Gary understands this technique well because it snagged him.

"I read on a message board that a company called Uniprime Capital found the cure for AIDS. That was in July 1999, and shares were trading for around $6.50. I thought it was quite a bargain for a company that cured AIDS, so I sold some of my big company stocks and bought 1,200 shares for $7,800."

Today it's worth twenty bucks. Uniprime ended up being a Las Vegas car dealership with a cutting-edge AIDS research subsidiary under the label "New Technologies & Concepts." New Tech & Con—emphasis on the con—was headed by Alfred Flores, the main force behind a series of false press releases announcing the miracle cure. Flores is not your typical medical researcher. During the time of the breakthrough discovery, he was in a Colorado prison for conspiracy to commit murder. Other than that, Uniprime was clean as a whistle.

Add this tip to the hundreds you may glean from these pages: Be skeptical of medical miracles originating in prison. Gary learned his lesson. "Whenever I see a stock idea, I conduct thorough research. I didn't know anything about Uniprime except what I read on the message boards. Greed got the best of me and I paid the price. But I also wisened up. Now, if I haven't read a company's financials, I'm not interested. People online can check financials at the 10-K Wizard."

> **10-K Wizard**

The Tale of Tokyo Joe

For true insult-to-injury fraud, how about paying a service to pump a stock? Many such services promise returns of 200 percent a year and cost $600 a month. Members receive daily e-mails telling them what to buy and when to sell and how fast to move. The trouble is, it's exhausting and few people do as well as the services claim. If you buy the second the buy e-mail arrives and sell the second the sell e-mail arrives, you might achieve a 20 percent return. But most people miss by a few hours and see those returns become losses. As my earlier example of running Wade Cook's numbers made clear, unendingly extraordinary returns are not possible. Remember starting with $1,000 and becoming a trillionaire within ten years on Wade Cook's money machine system? Well, a promise of 200 percent annual returns is no more believable. It would turn your $1,000 into $59 million in ten years.

The SEC investigated a service run by a guy named Tokyo Joe. His name alone should be enough information to convince you of the service's inability to further your financial future. In case it's not, let me reveal a bit more. His name isn't really Tokyo Joe, it's Yun Soo Oh Park and his service is called Société Anonymé. He started it in June 1998 with 280 members paying between $100 and $200 per month. By early 2000 there were more than 3000 members putting Park's monthly income at more than $300,000. His hobby? Buying Lamborghinis.

I could convey the details of the SEC complaint against Société Anonymé in my own words, but I think reading it straight from the source will be more convincing and better serve to keep you firmly away from such outfits. The following is taken from SEC Litigation Release No. 16399, filed on January 5, 2000:

> Specifically, the Complaint alleges that Park, a resident of New York, New York and the sole shareholder of Société Anonymé, provides investment advice over the Internet, including stock picks, to his clients, largely members of an Internet day trading community who pay $100 to $200 per month to Société Anonymé for the privilege of receiving his advice. Park provides such advice via his own web site, known as "Tokyo Joe's", via e-mails to subscribers of his stock recommendations, and via a real time chat room within his web site where he discusses his picks and other investment matters in more detail.
>
> The Complaint alleges that Park has engaged in a scheme to defraud by trading ahead of his recommendations and has obtained substantial profits from such activity. The Complaint alleges that Park regularly buys shares of a stock before recommending that Société Anonymé members buy the same stock. He then pumps up his members' interest in his upcoming recommendations by sending messages typically describing his picks as a sure thing or something he expects to double. When he identifies his pick of the day, many Société Anonymé members purchase the stock, driving up the stock's price and volume. Park then quickly sells the same stock during this buying flurry at a profit, often entering sell limit orders within minutes of his buy recommendation. Park fails to adequately disclose his prior ownership of a recommended stock, and his intent to sell his shares while he simultaneously recommends the purchase of such shares.
>
> The Complaint further alleges that Park attracts new Société Anonymé members and recruits current members to follow his recommendations by posting numerous effusive testimonials as well as false and misleading performance data on his web site. Specifically, the Complaint alleges that his performance data includes winning trades he did not actually make, erroneously reports his actual trading profits or losses and fails to include losing trades

and other trades necessary to make such performance data not misleading. Finally, the Complaint alleges that, in at least one instance, Park indirectly received compensation from the issuer of a stock he recommended without disclosing his receipt of that compensation.

The Complaint seeks the entry of an order of permanent injunction against Park and Société Anonymé, and ancillary relief in the form of disgorgement of Park's ill gotten gains plus prejudgment interest and the imposition of civil monetary penalties.

In March 2001, the SEC settled the case for $754,630. Park and Société Anonymé consented to avoid violating the antifraud and other provisions of the federal securities laws.

It looks like the Société wasn't Anonymé enough, at least not to escape the SEC's Scrutiné. It hardly seems necessary to review the reasons you should not join a club like this, so I won't.

I will, however, mention that internet stock fraud is on the rise. The SEC's internet complaint email address (enforcement@sec.gov) receives over 500 messages a day. When the address was first offered in June 1996 it received 10. The most common complaint involves email pushing obscure stocks.

> www.sec.gov
> enforcement@sec.gov

Be alert when you go online. Be alert when glossy mailers arrive on your desk. Be alert at all times and be careful with your money. Lots of people want it.

The Risks You'll Happily Avoid

Now you know that the stock market brings opportunity and risk. No big surprise, I hope. But some people see only the risk and opt to invest their money outside the market in things they consider safer.

I'm afraid I have unhappy news. The financial world outside

the stock market is also filled with slippery floors and sharp objects. It too threatens hearth and home and leers through the windows of your softly lit office. Frequently, investments outside the stock market lose your money or make you work much too hard for lower profits than stocks would have produced.

Let's look at some common non-stock investments that you can happily avoid by putting your money in stocks.

Real Estate Headaches

"The best thing about stocks," Ron Moesle told me, "is that they never call you in the middle of the night. They never break. They never skip town. They're not surrounded by plants that grow, and they're not covered by roofs that leak, and they don't produce any trash. They're printed on a statement that arrives in the mail each month and their numbers get bigger through the years."

Ron Moesle is a 67-year-old former Gallo wine salesman who lives in San Jose, California. He retired from Gallo when he was just 50 and has lived off his investments ever since. He's a successful do-it-yourself investor who's followed the path so many find appealing, namely, early retirement. Among Ron's investments are twelve real estate properties around the Bay Area. All the mortgages are paid on the units, which range from single-family homes to fourplexes. You would think that somebody with such a portfolio of property would sing loudly the praises of real estate. Think again.

"Stocks are a lot easier," he told me. "Real estate can be sort of a nuisance. I figured out that if you buy real estate you need to live down the street or a few blocks away. Don't live in San Jose and buy property in Los Angeles or another faraway city. You can't easily fix the water heater or the roof or paint the place. You shouldn't hire out the work, either, because you'll end up spending too much. I only pay for the huge stuff that's impossible to do on my own, like the sewer line."

That's what you'll be facing when you own investment property. The dream of sticking tenants in your building and collecting a monthly rent check that's 20 percent larger than your mortgage with no hassles along the way is just that—a dream. For most real estate owners, property management is a full-time job.

Even if you get a place with low maintenance requirements like a cement home surrounded by rock garden landscaping, you still have to collect rent every month. Dick Sherman, a native of southern California who's been buying real estate since 1951, says that's the main problem. "I'm always messing around with my properties. Maintenance and dealing with people take up all my time. The main problem is collecting money, the rent. Even people you think you can trust turn out to be trouble. I rented an apartment to a woman who worked as a paralegal and seemed like a sure bet. She's never paid on time, not even one month accidentally." He sighed. "In real estate, making 10 percent a year is doing well." That's less than the historic rate of return in the stock market, leading me to conclude that if underperforming the stock market is doing well in real estate, you might as well stick with stocks and avoid all the headaches. Besides, most do-it-yourself investors manage their money from home. Owning your home is the only real estate investment you need. It appreciates, benefits from leverage, and doesn't bring tenants that don't pay. Living in a home you own and putting your remaining investment money into the stock market is a good plan.

What's that you say? You don't own your home yet? Find some good stocks and in a few years you will.

Limited Profit Partnerships

Now we enter the land of really bad investing. One of the ways to reduce your risk investment is to save one of your most valuble resources—your time. Sounds tempting, doesn't it? That's how the idea of limited partnerships grabs so many people. You'll crack your knuckles and break pencil leads and kick things in your garage after joining one.

"It always sounds great," complains Sal Sandoval of Santa Fe, New Mexico. "They call you on the phone, those brokers, and they start talking tax benefits. They say how as a limited partner you don't have to do anything but sit back and send in the money. The general partner will handle all the details. He sure will, the details of losing everything."

Limited partnerships sprung up as a way to save on taxes. There's the general partner, whose official duty—despite appearances—is not to lose your money but rather to manage the project. Then there are the ~~suckers~~ limited partners who are supposed to receive income, capital gains, and those tantalizing tax benefits. Public partnerships are sold through brokers for minimums of $5,000, while private partnerships are put together with fewer than 35 limited partners who usually pony up more than $20,000 each.

Most limited partnerships handle things like real estate development, heavy equipment leasing, oil and gas exploration, movie deals, and research. The offers make you feel like a tycoon. "Yes, ma'am, you can be the owner of a sparkling new apartment complex with guaranteed rental income and a resale value at least four times the cost of development." Better than being part of a landlord team is being an oil baron. "It's the stuff that makes the world go round, no way to lose. We'll be drilling not just one, but several wells. That way we've got all the bases covered in case the first one doesn't hit oil. You take a look at the prospectus, and don't worry about all those warnings and that gibberish about conflicts of interest. The SEC makes everybody print those scare paragraphs. Hey, this is America. No risk, no reward, right?"

Right, and like Sal you might just decide to take that risk and become a proud limited partner in an oil deal. "It really did sound like a no-miss proposition," he remembers. "I'd been in the army with the guy putting the deal together, so I felt I could trust him. He was excited that the general partner's last name was Gretty. 'Sounds a lot like Getty the oil billionaire, doesn't it?' he said. 'If he doesn't know about oil then nobody does. He's already got three wells drilled and the first two are pumping enough oil to put you in the black even if nothing else goes right. The other seven wells are icing on the cake. *Lots* of icing!' I told him I couldn't afford a full unit at $20,000, and he said that was no problem. Mr. Gretty wanted friends and family to be able to take advantage of this unprecedented opportunity, so for me an exception would be made and I could buy a quarter of a unit. Only $5,000 out of pocket. I paid and became a limited partner."

You can guess how it went from there. The brilliant Gretty, who purportedly had oil flowing in his veins from birth, could not find enough black gold among all ten wells to change the oil in a school bus. The letters to Sal came less often and from different people each time. He stopped hearing from the army friend altogether, until he resurfaced one day with another investment opportunity. "I told him I was too busy managing my oilfields to consider another investment," Sal said.

Forget limited partnerships. If you want to be an oil baron, buy stock in or Exxon Mobile or ChevronTexaco. If you want to be a movie millionaire, buy stock in Blockbuster or Disney. If you want some heavy equipment action, buy stock in Caterpillar or Deere. The *limited* in limited partnerships refers to your profit, not your risk.

Becoming a Losing Lender

Banks are good at lending money; you're not. Lending investments include U.S. Treasury Bills, bonds, certificates of deposit, and savings accounts. All worthless unless you're a bank. Some conservative investors who just want to protect what they already have can put lending investments to good use, but most individual investors are looking to grow their money. They don't have so much that they spend their days looking for ways to protect it.

I taught a seminar in San Francisco where I met a woman named Nadaliana. Her hair was crow-black down to her waist and she wore carnival-colored clothes and jewelry that reflected light when she moved. For all her apparent wildness, she didn't employ one ounce of risk in the way she managed money. Nadaliana told me that in early 1995 her friend had convinced her to buy stock in "that chewing gum company."

"Wrigley?" I asked.

"Yeah, that's the one. So I did, a lot of it, at $42. Not two weeks went by before it dropped to $40 and I had to sell just to keep my sanity. I've kept that money locked up in a CD at Bank of America ever since. I never need to look at the stock market prices again because I know my money's safe. You should remember that, Mr. Kelly, when you go telling people they should put their money in stocks."

I have remembered, but not the way she wanted me to. I checked the price of Wrigley in early 1995 and saw that it had indeed been bouncing around $40 just as she said. By Spring 1998, the price reached $100. That would have been a 150 percent gain in three and a half years for Nadaliana had she stayed put. Instead, she earned around 5.5 percent in that safe Bank of America CD. If

$10,000 had been the amount she considered to be "a lot," then it would have become $25,000 left in Wrigley stock. In the CD, it became just over $12,000.

Millions of people have bank savings accounts, and that's too many. Checking accounts I can understand. It's not money that's supposed to grow anyway. It's money to spend. But savings accounts? Come on. How "safe" is that FDIC insurance when the money is guaranteed to never grow? Not very. In a way it's the riskiest investment of all when you have a long time frame. You won't reach any financial goals in a savings account, so you have chosen an investment with a 100 percent chance of failure. Is that the kind of risk you can afford to take?

The savviest independent investors laugh at banks, that is, unless they're bankers, in which case they love people like Nadaliana who are willing to lend them money for laughably low returns while the bank puts it in higher-returning places. Some of the shrewdest do-it-yourself investors I know make their living running banks. I've noticed something interesting about them. They run the bank and they gladly accept money from their customers, but their own investments aren't sitting in a bank CD. Worth noting, don't you think?

Bank accounts aren't the only low-returning lending investments. I recently hung a chart in my office that shows various asset classes from a $1 starting point in 1925 to their value in 1997. Small company stocks grew to $5520, large company stocks to $1828, long-term government bonds to $39, Treasury Bills to $14, and inflation to $9. Think hard and decide which path you'd like your long-term money to walk.

Getting Flimflammed

It's tough to argue that fraud is ever a wise investment, so I'm assured of being right when I say to avoid it. But no matter how foolish money scams look on paper from afar, they continue to blindside new people every year. "I don't get taken by scams," you might be saying to yourself. "This section doesn't apply to me." Then again, you might be nodding your head as you remember your own financial foolishness. Don't get too cocky. Perhaps your time has yet to come.

Prime Bank Securities

For instance, you could find yourself clucking your tongue one morning as you read the newspaper story about a grandmother who lost her retirement savings on a junk-bond deal. "She should have known better," you say confidently as you reach for the envelope containing a prospectus on prime bank securities. Who in the world would buy junk bonds when they could buy prime bank securities instead?

Who knows, but one thing we do know is that you're about to be just as suckered as the grandmother. Prime bank securities don't exist. They sound good no matter how they're pitched. If not for that tiny sticking point of not existing, they'd make fine investments.

A fine investment was exactly what Phyllis Granata of Reno, Nevada, wanted. "I'd been looking for a safe place to put money that would perform better than my bank CDs." That's when the envelope arrived in the mail. "It looked very official, on stationery like you expect from a bank, beautifully embossed. It offered an investment in revolving credit guarantees that it said were debt obligations guaranteed by prime banks. I asked an investor friend what they meant by prime banks and he said usually that means the world's one hundred biggest. Well, criminey, how could you go wrong with that?"

You could go wrong if there is no such thing as "revolving credit guarantees" or "prime bank securities" or "letters of credit" or any other way such phantom securities are presented. In this case, Phyllis's money went to the company making the pitch and that was that. She never received anything in return, and the company had long since packed off with its freshly cashed checks by the time she called to inquire.

New Utopia

Speaking of things that don't exist, here's a good one: New Utopia. The SEC discovered one Prince Lazarus Long, a.k.a. Howard Turney, selling bonds and currency to finance the construction of a country called New Utopia. Anybody lucky enough to get in on the deal was guaranteed a return of at least 200 percent and citizenship in the mysterious country. Millions were needed because New Utopia would rise from the Caribbean on enormous cement platforms built on a submerged landmass 115 miles from the Cayman Islands. The investment program's website logged over 100,000 hits before the SEC shut it down in April 1999. Prince Long denied all charges and said the SEC was conducting a "witch hunt." As bizarre as this one seems, it did attract some investors.

Pyramid Schemes

The pyramid scheme is an old standby that's still popular today. You too can fork over your money to an outfit that will use it to pay earlier investors their promised returns. If you're early enough in the game, you come out ahead. If not, you're the sucker.

We have Charles Ponzi to thank for this ingenius strategy. He was an Italian immigrant living in Boston in 1919 when he convinced investors to buy what he called "international postal reply coupons" for a 50-percent return in 90 days. Tens of thousands of investors contributed to a total haul of around $15 million. According to one recollection, "Money poured in so fast that his employees could hardly count it."

Ponzi opened branch offices and moved into a mansion. He took the money from newcomers and used it to pay the promised 50 percent returns to existing investors. Thrilled at getting their money, investors told their friends about the opportunity and even more money flowed in. Ponzi was rich and famous for a year, then the bottom fell out when he couldn't find enough newcomers to pay the money owed to existing investors. He ended up broke and in jail.

But Ponzi's legacy lives on. In October 1999 the SEC charged Mark Drucker with running a daytrading ponzi scheme to the tune of more than $6 million. True to form, he paid original investors with the money raised from newcomers. Meanwhile, his daytrading methods consistently lost money, $630,000 in 1999 alone. The money from his newest investors paid earlier investors and funded some rip-roaring house parties.

There's no end to the ways you can vaporize your money. Here's some foolproof advice that will serve you well in life: Never buy prime bank securities; don't fund fictitious countries being built on the ocean; and stay away from outfits that use your money to pay off earlier investors. Make sure you know what you're getting into.

And as long as I'm at it, don't start any chain letters.

Do-It-Yourself Investor Tools

When you first sit down as a do-it-yourself investor, you're revved up to make money. You'll see that stocks are the best place to start as they did terrifically well in the 1990s and pretty darned well over longer periods of time. But they occasionally hit rough spots like 2000 when the Nasdaq fell 39 percent. You might get excited and spring for shenanigans like the latest version of The Winning System. Stop, drop, and roll because perfect investments don't exist. Avoid investments outside the stock market too. They don't perform as well, often require too much work, and are higher risk.

Chapter Recap

Here's a rundown of what you learned in this chapter.

- **Stick with Stocks:** From 1997 to 2000 CMGI stock gained 14,000 percent, Yahoo 7500 percent, JDS Uniphase 6,000 percent, and eBay 3,000 percent. After reading that, it should be a simple conclusion to put your money in stocks. They're watched by the Securities and Exchange Commission, which adds a level of safety. They're run by professionals trying to grow the companies and make money for you, the shareholder. It doesn't always work. No guarantees, no way. But over time the market has returned around 11 percent a year.

- **In Good Times and Bad:** The Nasdaq fell 39 percent in 2000 while eToys, NaviSite, and CMGI ended the year off their 52-week highs by 99.4 percent, 98.6 percent, and 96.6 percent, respectively. From March 10, 2000, to April 4, 2001, the Nasdaq lost 68 percent. The market does that occasionally, which is why it's best used for your long-term money. Shooting for short-term gains is a lot like shooting craps.

- **The Winning System:** The Winning System is a fool's dream. It doesn't exist, so you might as well stop looking for it. Anybody who claims they can consistently double your money in three months is either untrustworthy or bad with a calculator. Fancy versions of The Winning System, such as the Elliott Wave Theory, attempt to explain the stock market's every movement with official-sounding terms. But for all the grand supercycles, minuettes, and sub-minuettes touted by such theories, they still aren't able to say where the market's headed tomorrow.

- **Stock Market Fraud:** You may want to sit down. Sadly, I've discovered fraud in the stock market. Some people use the Internet to pump up interest in a stock, then dump their shares after the price moves higher. It's called pump-and-dump. Some of those people have been nailed by the SEC, but others are sure to surface. Steer clear of outrageous claims. They usually lead to outrageous losses.

- **Skip Real Estate:** Real estate has proven to be a good investment over the years, but it requires a lot of work and usually ends up returning less than the stock market anyway. Real estate investor Ron Moesle puts it best when he says, "The best thing about stocks is that they never call you in the middle of the night. They never break. They never skip town. They're not surrounded by plants that grow, and they're not covered by roofs that leak, and they don't produce any trash. They're printed on a statement that arrives in the mail each month and their numbers get bigger." Owning your own home and putting your other money in stocks is a good balance to strike.

- **Avoid Limited Partnerships:** Limited partnerships are almost always a joke. Choose how you want to lose your money. Will it be commercial land development, equipment leasing, oil and gas exploration, movie deals, or research? Regardless, your limited share of the partnership will make the general partner rich while the investment goes nowhere because there's no oil, the movie stinks, and the research turned up worthless information.

- **Don't Lend Money:** You'll never make any money in bank accounts, and bonds are boring. So forget about these and other so-called lending investments if you're trying to get ahead.

- **Don't Get Flimflammed:** Fraud? Two words: avoid it. Never buy prime bank securities; don't fund fictitious countries being built on the ocean; and stay away from outfits that use your money to pay off earlier investors. These and other scams snag people every year.

Resources from This Chapter

Here are some ways to protect yourself from bad people in the money world. Always be on guard and use these weapons to defend your fortune.

- **10-K Wizard:** 10-K Wizard provides one of the easiest ways to see a company's latest financial reports. Taking a look at the official documents will help you avoid obvious mistakes like buying a company that doesn't exist or investing in a car dealership that has found the cure for AIDS. The 10kwizard site takes a company's ticker symbol and shows you the latest filings by date. You can even jump straight to specific sections of the documents, making research a snap. Contact Information: **www.10kwizard.com**

- **Securities and Exchange Commission:** The SEC is the investor's advocate. It watches your back and looks into anything shady. Its website shows the latest proceedings and has an enforcement section that summarizes investigations into certain stocks and brokers. If you've been defrauded or think you've found something fishy that should be checked out, visit the site and send a note.
www.sec.gov; **enforcement@sec.gov**

3 / The Calm Investor

Your mind should be at ease when investing. So let's discuss some issues that will help keep it that way.

First, we'll see that you might as well give up market forecasting because nobody knows where the market goes. Then we'll spend some time with Dr. Greed and Mr. Fear, the two hobgoblins that can easily get the best of you. Lastly, we'll see that sometimes you're going to lose money. But you know what? You won't care.

Now settle back and let me tell you about this interesting fellow I met.

The Rafter and the Dow

Gerald Kemmerling operates a whitewater rafting company in Ashland, Oregon. He fell in love with rafting after working a summer job as a guide to put himself through college. Now he's 39 and has owned his own company for fifteen years. He knew going into the business that nobody gets rich from rafting, though with proper money management he'd be able to do well. That's why he devoted a few evenings and weekends to studying money and the best places to keep it. Like others in this book, Gerald concluded that the stock market was his best choice.

"I can't watch the market day to day," he told me. "I'm too busy keeping equipment in top condition, training guides, and marketing my company. The last thing I wonder between phone calls is how the Dow is doing. It doesn't matter to me, and that's what has allowed me to keep my money in, regardless of what the market does. Looking back, that's been the right thing to do."

"When were the times you might have been tempted to sell?" I asked.

"Oh, probably back in 1990 and maybe in 1994. Obviously, April 2000 to April 2001 was rough." During each of those times, people worried that the good times couldn't continue. When the first signs of trouble showed up, like a bad week or month or year, people started saying it's time to get out. Gerald has been told things like "Don't be the last one holding the bag" and "Don't be the greatest fool." But he doesn't have time to place orders, and he doesn't feel qualified to guess what the market is going to do. So he just stays put and hopes for the best.

His profession has conditioned him to remain calm when everything around him is going haywire. Navigating whitewater rapids with scared guests makes the stock market's volatility appear boring. Even if you don't have the advantage of Gerald's training, you can learn a lot from his approach.

Nobody Knows Where the Market Goes

Market forecasting is a crummy job, and I'm continually amazed that anybody does it. I wish more of the experts had Gerald's honesty when he says, "I don't feel qualified to guess what the market is going to do." I've got news. Nobody's qualified.

I remember Japan being the hot market in 1990. It was downright obvious to anybody that the future of the world lay with that island country making great cars and electronics. The Japanese stock market returned an average of 22.5 percent a year during the 1980s, leaving Japanese companies flush and able to buy pieces of America like Columbia Pictures and Rockefeller Center. The Nikkei index ended 1989 at 38,916. The *Wall Street Journal* reported on January 2, 1990, that "even cautious observers call for the Nikkei index to end 1990 above the 45,000-point level." It ended at 23,849 and kept dropping. In October 1998 it closed at 12,880. The papers at that time were saying how horrible Japan was looking because of bad banking arrangements and a lingering recession. In 1999, several mutual funds investing in Japan returned more than 200 percent. The experts were wrong about when to get in and wrong about when to stay out.

The soothsaying is no more accurate in the United States. Starting in 1995, *Business Week* began each year by asking top market forecasters to predict where the Dow would close at the end of the year. In 1995, they thought it would reach 5,430. It closed above 6,430. . . .

	Market Forecasters	Actual Dow
1997	6,587	7,908
1998	8,464	9,181
1999	9,567	*well above* 11,000

Why bother?

One of the most infamous bad calls came from John J. Raskob, a financier in the early 1900s whose investment trust delivered a 22-percent average annual return for more than twenty years. He was interviewed in the August 1929 *Ladies' Home Journal* and said, "Everybody ought to be rich." He suggested that people should invest $15 per month in the market on margin. His reasoning will sound familiar to anybody who followed the financial press in the late 1990s and first two months of 2000:

> The common stocks of this country have in the past ten years increased enormously in value because the business of the country has increased. It may be said that this is a phenomenal increase and that conditions are going to be different in the next ten years. . . . In my opinion, the wealth of the country is bound to increase at a very rapid rate.

The timing of Raskob's comments couldn't have been worse. The stock market peaked in late August, then declined in September and early October. Still people continued speculating, many with borrowed money as Raskob suggested. The first day of panic came on October 24 when nearly 13 million shares changed hands. Banks tried to restrain the panic by purchasing blocks of stock, but they couldn't hold the market up for long. On October 29, "Black Tuesday," 16 million shares were traded as the market collapsed. Over the next three years, the market would lose 80 percent of its value, more than 10,000 banks would fail, and unemployment would reach 25 percent.

Yet, Raskob was no moron. His performance up to that mistimed interview was spectacular. His financial acumen helped start General Motors and DuPont, two of the finest companies of the day and still among the world's best. He was a smart guy who had done remarkably well in the very market he was forecasting. Even a man with his pedigree couldn't have been more wrong.

Which brings us back to the annoying conclusion we can't seem to escape, that nobody knows where the market goes. Let's take a peek at three sure things that studies have revealed about stock market forecasting.

Three Sure Things of Forecasting

First, the market does not always do what it did in the past. That makes research pretty tough. When all the indicators on somebody's computer screen say that whenever the market has risen this much it has always dropped 20 percent, they will share that insight boldly with investors. But the past has little bearing and *this* time the market might keep going another 10, 20, or 200 percent.

Second, the market rarely behaves as it should. There was a time when investment experts warned against owning a stock with a P/E greater than 20.

> *P/E:* The price/earnings ratio tells you how much you're paying for a company's earnings. A stock selling for $40 that earned $2 last year has a P/E of 20. The higher the P/E, the more expensive the stock.

That was considered the expensive mark. These days, people assume something is wrong with a stock that sports a P/E below 20. It shows low demand and therefore a company that's not doing anything interesting. Our children, should they become investors, might look back on the P/E ratios of top companies in the late 1990s and shake their heads in amazement that people were ever willing to pay so much for a stock. "Some of the companies didn't even *have* earnings," they will say with bewilderment. Yet, as I write this paragraph in March 2000, Yahoo stock trades at $190 with a P/E of 1652, has risen 780 percent in the past 18 months, and is up 4 percent today. There were people saying Yahoo would define the Internet and that everybody should own the stock. There were others saying that, historically, it's a tulip. The former have been right so far. Maybe it'll be a tulip any day now. (UPDATE, April 2001: What a *lovely* tulip—Yahoo now trades at $11, has fallen 93 percent from its 52-week high, and is down 19 percent today.)

Third, understanding the market means understanding human beings, which means we might as well give up trying. Some human beings get married and have children and go to church. Other human beings get angry and buy guns and shoot people from the tops of buildings. Some humans feel sad when they see an animal killed on a road; other humans swerve to hit animals they see crossing a road. Some vote yes while others vote no. Some eat worms, some tan nude, some drive Jaguars, some can't leave their homes in the morning. Some don't have homes. There are weirdos everywhere and there are normals everywhere. Some think they can tell one from the other, some don't. Given that this group of undefinable creatures affects stock prices by changing its demand, don't you find it comical that anybody claims to know where the market is going? Heck, I can't even know when the car in front of me is going to switch lanes, much less whether the driver is going to stay in the stock market through the end of the week.

You're Not the Market

"When the market does go one way or the other, my investments don't always follow it anyway," Gerald told me later in our talk. "I'd hear on the radio that the Dow broke 10,000 or that the Nasdaq closed at a record high for the fifth straight session, and I'd look forward to getting my brokerage statement. It would show up and I'd be ahead maybe 2 percent or nothing or I might have even lost a little. Then I realized, I don't own any Dow companies. So much for that average. I don't own a whole lot of technology companies. So much for the Nasdaq. Even if the experts could call the direction of the market correctly, they're not saying a thing about the direction of my specific investments."

That's an excellent point. With the enormous array of choices available today, it's quite possible that many of your investments are not even in the United States, much less in one of the closely followed U.S. market indexes. So when your favorite guru says the market will rise or fall, you can immediately contain your emotional response by asking yourself, "Which market?" and then, "Will my investments participate in the movement of that market?"

As far as Gerald is concerned, market movement just doesn't matter. "It doesn't affect money I need for groceries tomorrow. I put my long-term nest egg in the market and I put it in good companies and mutual funds. Unless capitalism goes away, good companies will shine. In the final analysis I trust the people managing the companies I own more than I trust the people telling me what the market will do."

Choose the Type of Risk That's Right for You

Gerald has swapped the uncontrollable risk of market fluctuation for the controllable risk of choosing good companies run by good people. That's one way to manage risk. There will always be surprises, but good people will respond to those surprises and keep their companies pushing forward. Investing in such companies will allow you to relax in up and down markets, which is to say *all* markets. You will be comfortable with the prudent risk you've taken by investing in companies run by people who don't care when the Dow loses 3 percent, companies that will not declare bankruptcy because interest rates are rising, companies that make money year after year.

Good times come and go. Good companies remain. Invest in good companies with some time to wait and you're taking little risk. In fact history says you're smart.

Risky, Greedy, and Fearful

Financial markets involve risk and risk stirs our emotions. The two core emotions of investing are greed and fear, and they're coming after you the second you buy a stock.

We are greedy to make money and we fear losing it. Taken to the extreme, greed and fear cripple your portfolio. When times are good, greed makes you borrow money to buy more stock, put money in speculative investments, or demand immediate performance. When times are bad, fear makes you sell your investments at a loss, stay out of the market at an opportune time to buy, or nibble at a ripe investment when you should be devouring it by the pound.

Get a hold of yourself! Let go of your hair, step away from the brokerage statement. Remember Rudyard Kipling's promise that if you can keep your head when all about you are losing theirs and blaming it on you; if you can meet with triumph and disaster and treat those two impostors just the same; yours is the Earth and everything that's in it. What's more, you'll be one unusual son of a gun and just the kind of person who can take advantage of a market plunge.

Behavioral Finance

You can learn a lot by skipping the investment papers and reading about behavioral finance, which studies our actions related to money. The mental processes that steer us right in everyday life can wreck us in the market. For example, it's good to be proud of an accomplishment, and most of our triumphs come from our own hard work and determination. That tendency leads many investors to look at their performance in a runaway bull market and take credit for their success. In the 1990s the stock market was so good to so many people that it seemed half the country thought it could pick stocks for a living.

Sorry, that's just not the case. Experts in behavioral finance use a concept called "hindsight bias" to describe your belief when looking back on past events that you knew ahead of time they would happen. You knew Microsoft would be the best stock of the 1990s, you knew to avoid Japan, you knew that Internet stocks like Amazon.com would set records. The truth is, nobody knew. It's easy to know now that Amazon.com should have been part of your portfolio in 1997 and 1998. It's easy to know now that you should have put nothing in Japan during those years. But don't tell me what you knew about then. Tell me what you know about next year. Suddenly, it's not so easy.

There are plenty of people who happened to own Amazon.com among other Internet superstars during the right years and considered themselves geniuses. Some probably backed that decision with research and careful thought. Others just got lucky. There are a number of common aphorisms we can use to describe the success of the lucky ones. A stopped clock is right twice per day; the sun shines on a dog's back; the genius and the idiot roll the same dice; and so on. Getting lucky is not a sign of skill. The rational, risk-adjusted investor knows when she's been lucky. She did well over the past few years but never thought it would be this good and is properly amazed. She doesn't kid herself into thinking she's the next Warren Buffett, whose historic performance is legendary but whose return might have been less than hers recently. Lately the market has gone her way, that's all. Someday it won't.

You'd Rather Get Ahead Than Be Ahead

Various behavioral finance studies conclude that investors suffer from "loss aversion." We hate losing money more than we love getting it. Say you have $100,000 and I have $20,000. You're ahead. Your investments turn south a bit, and your 100k becomes 90k. Studies show that you would be quite upset, slamming the paper down on the table, grumbling about all the things you could have bought with that ten grand. A heck of a vacation, you say to yourself. A new Jacuzzi, perhaps. Lots of aromatherapy. I, on the other hand, did well and turned my 20k into 30k. I'm jumping for joy. "Honey, we're ten thousand richer today than we were last month!" I would exclaim. "We could take one heck of a vacation. Maybe we could put in a jacuzzi. Or how about a membership to the day spa?"

Notice that you're still far better off than I. You have $90,000 while I have a piddling $30,000. But you're down and I'm up, and that's what makes the difference in emotion. Humans crave improvement. We want to be better off tomorrow than we are today. Our built-in loss aversion, or hatred of losing money, leads us to be too careful in the short term. That limits our wealth over the long term. We should try to see volatility as the price we pay for long-term improvement. Tomorrow you might have less than you have today, but you have what you have today only because you were willing to ride out fluctuations yesterday. That's the logical side of you speaking. The emotional side of you tries to get a word in edgewise saying, "You idiot! You should have sold yesterday and locked in that 30-percent gain." You need to actively work to keep the emotional side of you out of your portfolio, just like the rest of us.

The worst part about letting emotions kick you out of the market is that those same emotions can keep you out. Remember, we hate losing more than we love winning. That means we are naturally skeptical of the stock market. Logically, we know that the odds are in our favor. The market has in the past gone up twice as often as it has gone down. There's no guarantee that it will maintain that record in the future, but what else do we have to go on? Nothing. As the only evidence available to us, I'd say two-to-one odds in favor of a rising market are pretty convincing.

But there you are looking at your $90,000 and thinking of the 10-percent loss. There I am looking at my $30,000 and thinking of my 50-percent gain. Behavioral finance studies show that some interesting tendencies will follow our emotions. You're angry; I'm happy. You feel had; I feel triumphant. You're ashamed; I'm proud. You don't tell your spouse what has happened. In fact, you don't tell anybody. You start thinking that maybe a nice savings account would be a better way to go. The more you think about that vaporized ten grand, the more you kick yourself for ever investing in stocks. Who can call 'em? Nobody! It's a giant crapshoot, and only the bigshots on Wall Street are getting ahead.

You take a hesitant peek at your portfolio the next day and it's down the tiniest sliver, say a quarter of a percent. "That's $225!" you shriek. Enough's enough. Will the bleeding never end? You sell everything and swear to yourself that you will never squander the family fortunes again. How dare those financial-planning eggheads show you mountain charts of the market's past performance and the way it recovers from a downturn. Not with your money it won't! This time it's different. The market saw some glory days but they're over. It's nothing but bear from here on out. I, on the other hand, am the king of my world. There are no market uncertainties for me. I can pick 'em any day of the week! Career? Hah! Who needs a career when you are The World's Greatest Stock Investor? I spend hours looking over my 50-percent gain and after a while I ask myself a question. If I can achieve a 50-percent gain, why not 60 percent? It took me a year to gain 50 percent. Why not try to get my 60 percent in six months? Historic returns of 10 percent are for numbskulls. The World's Greatest Stock Investor doesn't think historically, and he doesn't confine himself to annual rates.

To achieve these newfound performance goals, I turn my attention away from the solid companies and mutual funds that have served me so well and toward speculative investments. As a matter of fact, why stick with stocks at all? Commodities and options are where it's at. Leverage, margin—I want it all.

And another thing. If anybody's got a stock tip, I want to hear it. I'm out to cream everybody and I've got to be in the hottest segment of the market every day of the week. If it changes daily, I'm trading over. No price is too much to pay either. I don't care about annual reports or what companies have planned. I want to know what the next press release will say and I want excitement! If a tip is good enough I'll put nearly all of my money into that investment. Diversification is for losers who don't trust their own trigger finger. I'm not one of those losers, and this isn't my grandfather's stock market. It's different this time with a different set of winners, and by God, I'm one of them.

You're in a state of despair. I'm in a state of euphoria. The market, which couldn't care less about either of us, changes course. Your $90,000 is now locked safely in a savings account and you miss the 20-percent recovery that would have put your fortune at $108,000. My $30,000 is now bet evenly on just three investments: a commodities contract on lumber, a penny stock for a company that almost has FDA approval on a drug that permanently eliminates bad breath, and a new computer chip manufacturer being billed as the next Intel. The lumber contract loses the whole ten grand. The penny stock misses FDA approval and declines by 45 percent. The next Intel hits a snag in the construction of its new fab and drops 30 percent. My once-proud $30,000 becomes $12,500.

Our emotions spun us out of control. You allowed fear to control you; I allowed greed to control me. You missed the recovery of your investments by fearfully exiting a fluctuating market. I vaporized my gains and much more by greedily pursuing instant riches. Markets recover and there are no instant riches. You and I are both aware of those facts. If we can control our feelings, we'll master the uncertainties of the market and keep a steady course upward over time.

A good first step is understanding how you feel about financial risk. Reading will help you define your feelings toward investing and let you know you're not the only one facing financial turmoil. A good primer on behavioral finance is *Why Smart People Make Big Money Mistakes*. I like *Mind Over Money* as well. The author helps you match your own temperament to a portfolio that suits you. Also consider *Investment Psychology Explained* and *Profits Without Panic*. The former is a collection of top writing on behavioral finance. The latter presents an approach called "psychonomic" investing that attempts to balance your internal personality market with the external stock market.

Investment Psychology Explained
Mind Over Money
Profits Without Panic
Why Smart People Make Big Money Mistakes

But who needs books when one quote says it all? Asked what the market will do tomorrow, J. P. Morgan replied, "It will fluctuate." Expect that, get your emotions in order, and you'll never be disappointed.

Your Fluctuating Fortune

A popular investment adage is that now is always the most difficult time to invest. It's true. Hindsight bias can't guide you, market forecasting has proven unhelpful. It's you and your money and a market that is as indifferent toward your financial goals as the weather is to your scheduled picnic.

Which brings us to the culmination of this chapter about keeping calm. You know the market's direction is a mystery. You know you'll feel greed and fear as that mystery unfolds. The final stage of serenity is accepting that your personal fortune—not just the market—will fluctuate in value. If you accept these realities, then you can save one of your most valuable assets—your sanity.

The best investors are humble because they understand that they cannot control the market or the entire performance of their own investments. The best investors are resigned to a fluid financial picture with Tuesday possibly looking much worse than Monday, but perhaps better than Thursday. "I've spent time charting the value of my portfolio," explains Trent Riley of Joplin, Missouri. "Most of the time, it moves sideways with tiny spikes up and down. Every once in a while, though, it surges upward 10 or 15 percent in a short period, then plateaus again. Watching the pattern has shown me that selling when the value is up a tiny bit and hoping to buy again when it's down a tiny bit is terribly risky because I will probably miss out on the few short periods when most of my gains happen."

Don't Miss the Little Bursts

You've probably heard of the 80/20 rule. Employers claim that 80 percent of the work gets done by 20 percent of the workers. Law enforcement claims that 80 percent of the crimes are committed by 20 percent of the people. In my hamper, 80 percent of the smell comes from 20 percent of the socks. (Actually, I think it's even more lopsided than that, but you get the point.) In many areas of life, a small fraction creates a huge effect.

Trent's observation of his own portfolio has shown him what paid researchers have concluded about the market as a whole. Most of its gains happen in little bursts. If you miss those little bursts, you miss a lot. That's why you should stay in the market for the long term. "I've stopped charting my money," Trent says, "because the pattern kept repeating. It changes slightly but basically my money goes up and down."

Then why is he calm? "Because I don't invest money that can't fluctuate."

The Intelligent Risk Manager's Motto

Commit this to memory: Do not invest money that you can't afford to have fluctuate. If it must remain a constant value, put it in a money market mutual fund. This seemingly simple step works wonders in keeping you happy through turbulent times. Only the money that you're prepared to let weather the storm will get tossed about. "And a lot of the tossing will be downwards," adds Trent, as if he's looking over your shoulder as you read. "Not sickeningly downward, but chipping away one percent here, half a percent there until several days or weeks have gone by and you begin to feel like you've missed a tiny leak in your balloon. Someday, a big puff of air into that balloon will make your portfolio float high again. It might not happen right away, but it will happen."

Three Days per Year

I can back up Trent's conclusion with some evidence. A moment ago I used the well-known 80/20 rule to illustrate that most of the market's gains happen in small bursts. I understated the case. A University of Michigan study found that 95 percent of the market gains between 1963 and 1993 stemmed from the best 1.2 percent of trading days. That's only three days per year. You've got to be some kind of wizard to keep yourself out of the market every day of the year except those three.

Naturally, the calm investor who is humble and resigned to a fluctuating fortune has long ago given up predicting which three days they'll be. Instead, like Trent, he has stopped watching. "I am the world's leading expert on what the market will *not* do," Trent admits. "Now, when anybody asks how my portfolio is doing I tell them that it's bigger than it was three years ago, smaller than it will be three years from now. During that six-year period, it will be up, down, and all around but I won't care. It's supposed to do that."

Your Amorphous Money Glob

"My brother and I started investing about the same time," Trent remembers. "We hit a rough patch in the early 1980s, and he permanently changed the amount of money he left in the stock market. Ever since then, he's been kicking himself for missing out on the market of the 1990s. One way he rationalizes his decision is by constantly telling me that the big one is coming, the crash that will wipe out all the gains I've seen over the years. In summer 1999 he called and asked if I was bothered by the increasing volatility of the market. 'What increasing volatility?' I asked. He then read to me from an article in one of the financial papers that said in the past two years the market has seen three drops of 10 percent or more. I had to roll my eyes. I told him it's always been that way." Trent is right. In the 24 months ending in June 1999, there were in fact three declines of 10 percent or more. But bigger declines than that are routine for the U.S. stock market. Since 1960, a decline of at least 20 percent has happened every 4½ years on average. Overseas, they occur more frequently. Such declines will bite a sizable chunk out of your portfolio. In the 1973–74 bear market, the S&P 500 fell almost 50 percent over a period of 22 months. Personal portfolios tied up in the leading stocks of the day fell even more.

Being an investor means experiencing ups and downs. You're going to face them eventually. You might as well do it with grace. When tallying your net worth, lop 10 percent off the current value of your stock market portfolio. You know it's a shifting mass, an amorphous glob that sometimes expands and contracts like a giant money amoeba. So play it safe, and always take away that 10 percent just in case a decline comes out of the blue. Accept that market money is not the same as wallet money or bank money. As soon as you do that and you know it's going to get bigger and smaller during the course of a day, you'll be relieved. The glob is changing size, that's all. You should be careful what money you put into the glob because it will change size too. Because your personal investment glob is made of money that can fluctuate, you'll stay cool as a cucumber. Amass your glob wisely and let it ooze where it will. Your mind will remain serene because you know your fortune will change size. No big deal. Remember, the surest way to manage risk is to invest money that you can afford to have fluctuate. In the long run, that's how you'll come up a winner.

Do-It-Yourself Investor Tools

Keeping calm when the market flips out is a rare skill. It's easier when you've given up predicting the market's direction and accepted that your fortune will fluctuate.

Chapter Recap

Here's a rundown of what you learned in this chapter.

- **Nobody Knows Where the Market Goes:** Nobody can predict the direction of the market. None of the analysts, none of the media, none of your colleagues, not you, not me, nobody. The market doesn't always do what it has done in the past, which makes it tough to know what it's going to do in the future. Even when experts discuss the market there's no guarantee that the part they're discussing has anything to do with your specific investments. Predicting a stock's price is like aiming at a moving target on a shifting field on a cloudy day with a piece of dirt in your eye.

- **Controlling Dr. Greed and Mr. Fear:** Learning a little about investment psychology can help get your runaway feelings under control. Greed and fear are the hallmark emotions of investing. When you've made some money, you get overconfident and assume you can make lots more easily and start taking big risks.—GREED. When you've lost some money, you start thinking that you'll never get it back, and you hide in the corner with the light off while taking too little risk.—FEAR. Get your greed and fear under control and your performance will improve.

- **You Hate Losing More Than You Love Winning:** Here's another handy revelation from the world of investor psychology. You want to protect what you already have more than you want to make more. That means you'll feel like garbage when the market goes down but feel only mild contentment when it goes up. Know that in advance.

- **You'd Rather Get Ahead Than Be Ahead:** One more lesson from the shrinks—your overall financial happiness has more to do with the direction your wealth is taking than with your actual worth. A guy whose account goes from $30,000 to $50,000 feels great. A guy whose account goes from $30 million to $15 million feels lousy. It's ironic but if they met at a bar, the poor guy would be the one offering to buy a cheer-up drink for the rich guy. Of course, a rich guy getting richer would be the happiest jerk in the whole place.

- **Three Days per Year:** Give up trying to guess the market. A University of Michigan study found that 95 percent of the market gains between 1963 and 1993 stemmed from the best 1.2 percent of trading days. That's only three days per year. You're never going to correctly call them, so stay in for the long haul and relax. Only Coca-Cola knows which three days are the winners for any given year and—(wouldn't you know it?) they keep the list locked in the safe next to their secret recipe.

- **Occasionally You're Going to Lose Money:** Resign yourself to losing money now and then. Since 1960, the U.S. stock market has declined at least 20 percent every 4½ years on average. In the 24 months ending in June 1999, there were three declines of 10 percent or more. In 2000, the Nasdaq lost 39 percent. Don't put your grocery money in the stock market, or you might be serving croutons and tap water. Only invest money that can fluctuate.

Resources from This Chapter

It's a good idea to learn as much as you can about investor psychology so you're prepared when the emotions start heating up. Here are some good books on the subject.

- *Investment Psychology Explained: Classic Strategies to Beat the Markets* by Martin J. Pring (1992). This is a comprehensive look at market behavior that's best described by the author: "My purpose in writing *Investment Psychology Explained* was not to break new ground, but to bring together, in one volume, a distillation of the soundest wisdom and basic common sense on the subject of market psychology."

- *Mind Over Money: Match Your Personality to a Winning Financial Strategy* by John W. Schott (1998). You couldn't ask for a more qualified author for this title. John Schott is both a professional money manager and a psychoanalyst at Harvard Medical School. He looks at the damage caused by greed and fear, then builds your confidence with investment approaches that are ready-made for your own mind-set. No medications included, I'm afraid.

- *Profits Without Panic: Investment Psychology for Personal Wealth* by Jonathan Myers (1999). Here's the rundown on "psychonomic" investing, an approach that uses your personal priorities to best position your money. It's a balance between your internal market and the external market. Jonathan Myers claims that "once you begin to separate out these internal and external elements, it becomes easier to see the opportunities."

- *Why Smart People Make Big Money Mistakes—and How to Correct Them: Lessons from the New Science of Behavioral Economics* by Gary Belsky and Thomas Gilovich (1999). Too many rational people make irrational decisions when it comes to their money. This book looks at the reasons you invest, spend, and save as you do, then offers a bunch of ways to help you do it all better.

4 In the Oysters and Under the Rocks

You find pearls in oysters and worms under rocks. But not every oyster and not every rock produce such yields, so you won't know which ones until you start poking around. Sure, you can buy pearls for jewelry and worms for bait, but they're never as good as the pearls and worms you find yourself. Since one of your most valuable resources is time, you'll want to maximize your research rewards by reducing your amount of search time. Good investors do good research, and much of what they find is better than what they could buy from an advisor. Most research turns up nothing. Being willing to wait for a good discovery is the mark of a superb investor.

I've mapped out a path for the do-it-yourself researcher. In the beginning, you'll absorb everything, but sooner or later you'll get tired of it all and focus your research. Then you'll learn what to ignore altogether. After that you might want to try using a computer to cut down on research time. Finally, you'll learn a few ways to eavesdrop on what the pros are buying and selling.

All in due time. First, I'd like you to meet somebody who thinks like an investor.

Think Like an Investor

Norikazu Okuyama has lived in the United States for more than fifteen years, studying English and obtaining a Ph.D. in linguistics. He also teaches Japanese to Americans in the Los Angeles area. Prior to 1999 all of his money was invested in mutual funds targeting U.S. stocks. Then in late 1998 his eyes were opened to what he considered an unprecedented opportunity in his home country.

When you ask Norikazu what he does, he would answer that he's a teacher. But he's more than that. He's an investor. When somebody asks what you do, you too would answer with your profession—you're an accountant, a plumber, an advertising executive, a computer programmer. Whatever you do, it took years of education and training to become good at it, just as it has taken years for Norikazu to learn English well enough to teach in the United States. In other words, our profession is what produces our income, what brings money into our household. Few people define themselves as investors, yet we all are. If you are reading this from your home, then you are living inside an investment. Every class you take, every seminar you attend is an investment in yourself, your market value as expressed by what you can earn. With a little time you'll widen that perspective to think like an investor in every situation.

In Norikazu's case, one such situation was his trip to Yokohama, a city just south of Tokyo, to visit family. Norikazu couldn't believe the change that had swept across the Japanese population since his last visit two years earlier. "Japan had been in recession throughout the 1990s," he explained. "People went to work, came home, didn't spend money, and never considered investing in the market that had destroyed so much of their capital. I had given up hope of ever finding prosperity again in Japan. The wealth was in the United States."

But by watching those around him and paying close attention to the mood of his relatives, Norikazu noticed something important. "People were upbeat. They used more technology than the typical American. I don't think there's a pay phone left anywhere in Japan because everybody carries a tiny digital phone in their pocket. These days you see that in the States as well, but back then you didn't. I was impressed." Seeing a nation full of upbeat people using new technology caught Norikazu's attention. What kept it was a conversation with his cousin about retirement plans. "Up to that time, the Japanese weren't allowed to invest their retirement money. Companies ran pensions and provided set payment schedules. My cousin was excited because there was talk about Japan creating self-directed plans like the ones in the States. That would put people's money to work in the stalled Japanese stock market and, I thought, probably drive prices higher."

In a fun vacation to visit family, Norikazu kept his eyes peeled and his ears open and found a smart investment opportunity. When he returned to California, he conducted further research and decided that the new, small Japanese companies making the parts in those little phones and driving the growth of the Japanese Internet were a better bet than the familiar names like Toyota and Sony. He found a gem of a mutual fund that targeted exactly what he was looking for: Warburg Pincus Japan Small Company. How did he do? Not bad. In 1999 the fund returned 329 percent, yet at the end of the year Japan's stock market had still reached a level only half as high as its peak in 1989. Norikazu thinks that both his country and his investment have many happy years ahead, despite a rough 2000, which saw the fund fall 72 percent. His initial investment is up 20 percent even after the big dip, and Norikazu invested more money at the fund's cheaper prices.

That's what thinking like an investor is all about. Paying attention, drawing conclusions, and acting on those conclusions. Put your money to work. As Ben Franklin pointed out, "Money makes money, and the money money makes makes more money." Noninvestors on Norikazu's trip might have marveled at the bright lights of Tokyo, enjoyed sashimi, and been delighted at the punctuality of Japanese commuter trains. They would also have witnessed the widespread use of tiny phones and maybe detected optimism among the people. But they would have returned home with only several rolls of film and a rubber Samurai sword, but no thoughts of investing in mind. Meanwhile, Norikazu paid for his trip and a whole lot more by thinking like an investor.

Investment Info Everywhere

Take a look at the grocery store newsstand the next time you're buying yogurt. See how many business and investment publications are available. Here's a partial list from my grocery store and the newsstand across the street from where I shop:

Barron's	Global Investor, Inc.	Online Investor Magazine
Black Enterprise	Individual Investor	Red Herring
Bloomberg Personal Finance	The Industry Standard	SmartMoney
Business 2.0	Industry Week	Technology Investor
Business Week	Investor's Business Daily	Technology Review
Emerging Markets Quarterly	Kiplinger's Personal Finance	Upside
Family Money	Money	The Wall Street Journal
Fast Company	Mutual Funds Magazine	Worth
Financial Times		Your Money
Forbes		
Fortune		

Subscribing to all of them would cost you more than $1,000 per year and provide you with over 7,000 pages of reading per month. Want to know a secret way to reduce your investment costs thus your upfront risks? Visit your local library. In addition to the publications above, most libraries have expensive newsletters like Standard & Poor's *Outlook*, *Morningstar Stock-Investor*, and *Grant's Interest Rate Observer*.

Television and radio are even more pervasive than reading material. The locker room of my health club keeps a large screen TV tuned to CNN Financial Network. The men dry themselves watching stock quotes run across the bottom of the screen and listening to the talking heads. One time I heard a raquetball player shout, "Hey, I just made $2,000 washing my hair!" When I leave the health club to drive home, I listen to an investment radio program.

Magazines at the grocery store, television at the health club, radio in your car—it seems harder to get away from investment information than it is to find it. Which means that your initial job of absorbing everything is simple. Just put up your investment antenna and tune in.

The Everywhere Info Is Just Fine, Thanks

So now you're reading, watching, and listening to everything related to investing. You're constantly asking yourself, Where can I profit today? That's how it begins, at least. As you get better, you'll have your money already invested, and everything new that you find will be quickly compared to your current portfolio for an appropriate response, like "Um, I guess I'll just lie down on the couch for a while." Nine times out of ten the best course of action is no action at all. This is hard for a lot of people to accept. The art of investing is so often the art of vegging out while all hell breaks loose in the background.

But you do need to research your investments. You'll eventually tire of absorbing everything and want to concentrate your research because as an investor you're not using the media to be entertained. You're working. Sticky notes nearby, pad of paper open, and pen in hand, the investor concentrates on what he's reading. It's not just a story about a nifty new drug, it's about a public company with a certain amount of profit to be made. How many people suffer from the affliction cured by the drug? How close is the drug to FDA approval? What percentage of the company's income will the new drug represent? Most important, was the research for this drug conducted in a prison cell by a guy suspected of murder?

And then one day it dawns on you that your investment performance might improve if you just had access to better information. Thousand-dollar reports. Insider bulletins. The wink and nod kind of stuff that the bigshots in Manhattan read in their smoking clubs. You're suffering from Info Envy. It was an airport coach driver in Denver named Rory who first introduced me to Info Envy. I told him I'm a financial writer, a personal tidbit that brings out the investor in everyone. Rory assumed I have access to the wingtip corridors of Wall Street and said he felt stupid for getting all his ideas from one magazine. "I just read *SmartMoney* each month," he told me. "I'm sure there's better info available, but I haven't found it."

The Sugar Water Bulletin

Actually, Rory, neither have I. Research reports from institutions, some costing hundreds or even thousands of dollars, contain excellent information but rarely more than what an astute investor can gather from more common sources. Furthermore, you will hear it said—and I agree—that by the time information is printed in the regular media it's old news to the pros. Well guess what? Few of us are pros. If we were we'd be sitting in downtown offices reading expensive reports paid for by our firm. Instead, we're individual investors funding our own research efforts and conducting the research in spare moments between work and family.

That should not discourage anybody. If the only research readily available to the individual investor is old news to the pros, we'll take it. Despite the media's infatuation with short-term trading, most people make their money in the markets through a buy-and-hold strategy. Buy-and-hold does not require access to the latest information on a company. Besides, the regular media is pretty quick at delivering information. Think about it. What breaking research do you need to understand why the business model of Coca-Cola works? Is somebody going to conduct a taste test that proves once and for all that mainland Chinese require daily doses of Coke to function properly? That would be wonderful news for Coca-Cola shareholders, but it isn't going to happen. Coke is sugar water sold all over the world through one of the most comprehensive and persistent marketing campaigns ever. It continues to expand to new markets and maintain its popularity in old markets because it tastes good. I can't imagine pizza without a Coke. Others can't begin a movie without popcorn and a Coke.

Anybody who thinks for a moment knows that the business behind Coke is a massive one involving manufacturing, packaging, distribution, publicity, and so on. There are little developments along the way like a health scare in Europe or a bottling snafu or a discrimination lawsuit, but for the most part Coca-Cola keeps doing what it has done all along and will continue doing forever. In the words of former CEO M. Douglas Ivester in Coke's 1998 annual report:

> Our unparalleled business system was built by decades of investment, commitment, and faith. Businesses fixated on

the short term could have easily shunned the United States in the 1930s, Europe in the '40s, Latin America in the '70s, Africa in the '80s. This Company did not, and our success today demonstrates the virtues of taking the long view. It is ingrained in our culture: This Company has invested and grown during world wars, hyperinflation, and depression. In 113 years, volume has declined only 12 times, the last time 44 years ago.

What breaking research do you need? If kids in Belgium get sick from drinking Coke, perhaps the stock price will dip a few dollars. If Coca-Cola's market share in Japan increases by one percent, perhaps the stock price will rise a few dollars. Big deal. These are not the kinds of moves that should worry or excite anybody.

You don't need to subscribe to the $989 *Sugar Water Bulletin* to know what's up at Coca-Cola. Whatever is important enough to affect the share price in a meaningful way will be reported in the general press with sufficient time for the general public to react, and that includes health scares in Belgium and market share in Japan. Like Coke's steady business history, your profits in Coke stock will happen over months and years of steady appreciation. There will be surges and dips during those years, but you won't know when they're coming no matter what you read because, as I hope you'll recall, nobody knows where the market goes. Not even the good folks at the *Sugar Water Bulletin*. So you shouldn't seek split-second profits from expensive info.

Don't point to the one-day wonders among Internet stocks as proof to the contrary. All of us know somebody who knows somebody who made 500 percent in a day and claim they saw it coming. People have made overnight fortunes in Vegas too, but not you and not me. Most important, the flash, bang, boom kind of riches are just lucky breaks that involve far too much risk for the occasional reward they produce. They make for thrilling after-the-fact stories, but they do little to help you and me get ahead in the market.

So, back to Coke and your use of everyday information. The magazines you select from the grocery store as being the best for you will be fine. Just as the hammer does not make the carpenter, neither does the research make the investor. It's what you do with the research that counts. A proper analysis of a newspaper article is worth more than an improper analysis of a $1,000 whitepaper from a Wall Street institution. It may be obvious, but I still have to ask—Wouldn't you rather invest that $1,000 in the purchase of a stock than in research materials that may or may not produce valuable information?

The Headlines of Akamai

Let's look at an example that was the toast of the Internet in late 1999 and early 2000: Akamai Technologies. You might assume that reading blue suit reports from the likes of Morgan Stanley Dean Witter would give you inside info and turbo performance. Why surely, you think, the analysis provided by such a Wall Street firm, not to mention the timeliness of its report, would make it far more useful than sources the unwashed public reads.

Decide for yourself: Morgan Stanley released a report on Akamai in late January 2000 with the scholarly headline, "Going, Going, Gone—Akamai Knocks One Outta Here." The analysts were so overcome by the company's potential that standard English was deemed inadequate for description. Instead the report suggested that "moves into new businesses such as streaming media and application development can only be described as Akamai." According to the corporate backgrounder, *akamai* is Hawaiian for intelligent, clever, and cool. In the world of mundane information available to the masses, on October 1, 1999 (about four months earlier), *USA Today* printed the following in a large story about the quality of talent behind new Internet start-ups: "One example is Akamai, a year-old company that helps content move faster across the Net. Akamai lured former IBM and BBN Planet executive George Conrades to be its CEO and just got a $15 million investment from Microsoft."

Akamai Technologies went public in late October 1999. If you had read the *USA Today* article among the many others available in grocery store fare, you might have been looking to buy shares as soon as possible. The soonest you could have picked them up through a typical broker would have been at a price of $150, but let's be conservative and say you didn't get around to buying until the first week of November at $190. By the time the professional money managers read the Morgan Stanley report at the end of January 2000, they would have had to buy shares at $270. By then, your November purchase would have already appreciated 42 percent. (U P D A T E: Akamai finished the year 2000 at $21. On April 5, 2001, it hit $5.50 without having earned a penny in profits. The pros following Morgan Stanley's report lost 98 percent. How intelligent, clever, and cool.)

As you can see, the regular old media performed just fine in this area of fast-moving stocks. No need to pay extra for timely information. No need to pay extra for the supposed analysis by professionals. Your mind is all you can count on when processing the information that reaches it everyday. In this case, it would have been just fine to read the *USA Today* story and the Morgan Stanley report, check Akamai's earnings, and say, "No thanks."

And by the way, notice that I as a do-it-yourself investor was able to get my hands on the Morgan Stanley report. You'll be amazed at what the individual can accomplish with a few phone calls, Internet searches, and a carefully maintained network of fellow investors. You'll also be amazed at the number of times aggressively sought information turns up nothing more than the daily newspaper.

What Shall We Read?

It should be clear to you by now that it's not just the information that counts. It's how you use it, how you read between the lines, how you anticipate what's in store for the investment in question. That's as much art as science, but nothing will develop that art as well as practice with real-world information and real money.

So, where shall we go for the focused amount of information we need? To reduce your upfront costs so as to maximize returns, I suggest starting with *SmartMoney* and *Worth*. Each magazine serves up good stock and mutual fund ideas and holds itself accountable by monitoring the performance of its picks. *SmartMoney* is better at company news and market conditions, while the columnists at *Worth* are an all-star cast including Peter Lynch, Walter Russell Mead, Robert X. Cringely, Jim Rogers, and Andrew Tobias. In the newspaper category, there's no contest: read

> **Investor's Business Daily**
> **SmartMoney**
> **Worth**

Investor's Business Daily. It's a pure investment paper with loads of data you won't find anywhere else, like its "SmartSelect" stock rankings for earnings growth and price strength. It focuses its news on what an investor wants to know, not on what a business person wants to know.

There is a difference. The information you read in business papers like the *Wall Street Journal* and business magazines like *Forbes* and *Fortune* is intended for corporate managers. It's an eye on the competition, a look at new processes, and so on. It's not specifically about buying this company or selling that one. This is not to say that the information contained in business publications is useless. I just took you through an example of how *USA Today*, which is certainly not an investment publication, provided information that could have been turned into a profit with Akamai Technologies. Similarly, you will find plenty of profitable information in general business publications.

However, as a do-it-yourself investor you don't want to read everything. You want to choose carefully where to spend the limited amount of time you have for research. You will find more profit per page in *SmartMoney* and *Worth* than in *Business Week*, *Forbes*, or *Fortune*. You will find more profit per page in *Investor's Business Daily* than in the *Wall Street Journal*, *Barron's*, or *Financial Times*.

Now to the Internet. Yahoo Finance is hands-down the best place to monitor portfolios, see the averages, and catch top news stories. The site's stock and fund profiles are superb. Two factors set Yahoo apart from competitors: the site loads quickly and it's entirely free.

Beyond Yahoo Finance as your core research stop, visit CBS MarketWatch, Morningstar, SmartMoney, TheStreet, and Worldlyinvestor. For discussion boards, go to Motley Fool and Raging Bull. To see what other individual investors are buying along with the investors' performance history, go to ClearStation and iExchange. For charting, use Bigcharts. To buy professional reports, browse Multex. To read updates to this book and find additional resources related to what you learned in this book, visit my site at JasonKelly.com.

> **Bigcharts**
> **CBS MarketWatch**
> **ClearStation**
> **iExchange**
> **Jason Kelly**
> **Morningstar**
> **Motley Fool**
> **Multex**
> **Raging Bull**
> **SmartMoney**
> **TheStreet**
> **Worldlyinvestor**

Finally, let's talk a moment about newsletters. This places me in an awkward position because I publish one. Mine is called *The NeatSheet* and covers both mutual funds and stocks every month. Naturally, because I publish a newsletter, I find them to be valuable. But I won't lie to you and say that it's necessary to receive an expensive newsletter for superior investment performance. It's not. Every piece of info in newsletters is available elsewhere—I don't care how much the newsletter costs. To be sure, there are excellent newsletters on the market. They contain top quality writing, thorough analysis, and home-run investment picks. There are also duds that contain little more than what you'll find in the Sunday paper.

Tops among institutional publications are Standard & Poor's weekly newsletter, *The Outlook*; Morningstar's monthly newsletters, *FundInvestor* and *StockInvestor*; and Value Line's weekly newsletter, *The Value Line Investment Survey*. In the camp of newsletters dispensing the advice of a single figure, I suggest *Chartist, MPT Review, The NeatSheet,* and *No-Load Fund Investor*. Most newsletters will send you a sample issue for evaluation. Your goal should be to find a newsletter that tells you about the types of stocks and funds that you would have found on your own if you had more time. If you get just one or two good ideas from your newsletter per year, the subscription price becomes a moot point. Good investment ideas are worth thousands or tens of thousands of dollars. Most newsletters cost less than $300 per year, many less than $100.

> **Chartist**
> **FundInvestor**
> **MPT Review**
> **The NeatSheet**
> **No-Load Fund Investor**
> **The Outlook**
> **StockInvestor**

Learn What to Ignore

After you've gone through your phase of absorbing everything, then reduced your exposure to just the handful of sources that you find best, you will enter a stage of investment finesse where you purposely ignore information that doesn't pertain to your investments. Do-it-yourselfers carefully guard their time and free thought and, yes, their portfolios from whims of the moment. In our media-obsessed culture, it's easy to get sidetracked by a network's latest attempt to boost ratings. The talking heads forget by Friday what they were hysterical about on Tuesday and besides, three quarters of what they report is related to making money in the next 72 hours. I submit that skipping the hysterics altogether—and the talking heads as often as possible—will in the end serve most do-it-yourselfers far better than monitoring every media spasm.

One guy who has it right is Norm Linkins. He's been investing longer than I've been alive, and he's made enough to consider $100,000 positions play money. I'll never forget a call I received from him one day asking if I thought he should experiment with a tiny portion of his portfolio by putting it into an Internet mutual fund. "How tiny a portion?" I asked. "Just a percent or so," he replied, "around a hundred grand I suppose."

When a guy like that calls for advice, it's humbling. I learn as much from Norm as he does from me, and one of the interesting pieces of information he passed along is that he pays attention to very little in the market. "I never have understood most of the government statistics released every quarter. Some people get excited when nonfarm payrolls are released, and consumer confidence studies, and existing-home sales, and similar figures that mean so much to economists. To me, it's just mumbo jumbo."

To some, Norm's comments will come across as ignorant, the words of a happy-faced dart-thrower who happens to have gotten lucky along the way. Not to me. I think half the people discussing economic trends in the media don't know anything more about them than Norm, and even if they do it doesn't do any good. The fact remains: Nobody can consistently time the market.

Avoiding Risky Behaviors

Watching your portfolio too closely can lead to all sorts of trouble. Minute movements can take over the whole mental process until you see nothing but red and green arrows and flickering prices. Then you might engage in high-risk activity.

Do-it-yourself investors wiser than I have concluded that daily updates are too much noise. Among my favorites is Bill Lovins. He checks his portfolio once a month and makes any changes then. That's it. He deliberately does not receive a daily newspaper or watch television or listen to the radio. Just for kicks, he occasionally peeks at what happened during the past month while he's been happily oblivious. "Sometimes, I see that the value of my portfolio hit a point 10 percent lower than its current level. Other times, it's 10 percent higher. I never think that I should have bought more at the low or sold at the high. Life is for living, not for slicing numbers that way. The market has been generally good to me and I expect that to continue. How anybody can watch daily investment events is beyond me."

There's a special strength inherent in the investors who are quietly confident in their portfolios. Everybody's aware of it, even the people who are more skittish. I received an e-mail from reader Maria Salazar. She wrote, "I attended a meeting in August after a particularly bad few days in the market. I said to my friend, 'Can you believe how low the Nasdaq is going?' She looked at me and said, 'Oh, is it falling this week?' I was flabbergasted! 'Falling this week' was an understatement. Every website discussion board used the word *carnage*, and the daily reports said Greenspan was going to raise rates, and I even saw something about another Asian crisis on the horizon. And my friend was completely unaware. I told her the gory details and she said, 'It'll go back up.' That was it. And you know what made the whole thing maddening? She was right."

Don't Know and Don't Want to Know

The calm people usually are right. The adage that if you're not panicked, then you don't understand the situation doesn't often apply to investing. This detached interest in the market is not a trait peculiar to small-time independent investors. Warren Buffett himself fastidiously ignores short-term market behavior. He wrote in 1993:

> After we buy a stock, consequently, we would not be disturbed if markets closed for a year or two. We don't need a daily quote on our 100 percent position in See's or H.H. Brown to validate our well-being. Why, then, should we need a quote on our 7 percent interest in Coke?

Some investors go so far as to purposely ignore granular details about the companies they own. Most often, I find this trait among mutual fund investors who don't necessarily even care about the individual companies owned. They just make a call on the big picture and leave the details to the fund manager.

"I manage nurses in a big Los Angeles hospital," Cecille Recio told me. "I talk to doctors and hospital managers all day long. I know healthcare is a booming business because I see how much people spend and I see how quickly new treatments and equipment are being developed. But the truth is, I don't understand a lot of it. All I know is that there's money to be made in healthcare. So I put my retirement account into healthcare sector funds and even some biotech funds. They've done well over the years. I recently put money into the Janus Global Life Sciences fund because I like that it can invest in healthcare anywhere in the world. That's been the best performing mutual fund I've ever owned. I don't know what's in it and I don't want to know. It just does what it's supposed to do."

If you've ever read the annual report of a biotech company, you can probably relate to Cecille's feelings. It's tough for the lay person to figure out which human genome company is going to win, or which heart transplant procedure is going to prove most helpful, or which imaging machine is going to gain the most market share. Half the time, I don't even understand the words being used to describe the breakthroughs, much less their business potential.

But, like Cecille, you might have a general idea for a part of the economy that's going to do well. If you have limited time, it seems reasonable to me that you would buy a fund specializing in that sector. Possibly you've done some research, and you have a pretty good idea that a single company will prosper because of its field of operation. You might not understand everything there is to know about the company, but you see that it has a strong management team, a good product line, and a wide-open niche to occupy.

Don't listen to people who tell you that mutual fund investing is for sissies. Combined with a prudent amount of research, I find sector funds to be among the smartest ways for individual investors to make a buck. Take Cecille, for instance. Her occupation as a director of nurses in a hospital qualifies as excellent research in the healthcare industry. Her educated decision to invest in Janus Global Life Sciences proved astute and profitable. In 1999, the fund returned 61 percent compared to 21 percent for the S&P 500. In 2000, the fund gained 33 percent compared to −10 percent for the S&P 500. If those returns qualify as sissy investing, I'm wearing pink tomorrow.

I've heard it said that half of being smart is knowing what you're dumb at. Likewise, half of being an informed investor is knowing what you *don't* need to know. For Norm Linkins, it's hard economic data from Washington. For Bill Lovins, it's the daily movements of his portfolio. For Maria Salazar's friend, it's the volatility of the market itself. For Cecille Recio, it's the details of the healthcare industry. Your investment performance will not improve by overloading your mind with details that it can't or doesn't want to understand, or that create emotional responses that lead to high-risk behaviors. Overload will only frustrate you and discourage the research that would actually help you. Learn *what* to ignore, then *ignore* it.

The Siren Song of Investment Software

With so many people talking about technology, you might think it's time to buy investment software. "Get with the program. Work smarter, not harder." That kind of thing.

Like the sailors of Greek mythology, you could be lured to destruction by sweet song. Don't think for a second that software will guarantee your success as an investor. Computers have opened new ways for individuals to research their investments, but the interpretation of the data is still up to you. The smart investor with a newspaper is more potent than the fool with a keyboard. Then again, an investor at a conference told me he's found some of the best stocks in his portfolio by using software and went further to claim that he couldn't have done so without it. I asked how long he held his stocks. "Depends," he replied. "Sometimes as long as a month."

Dashed on the Rocks of Daytrading

In that story there lies a clear lesson. Most investment software caters to short-term investors and daytraders. I found evidence of that in an ad for a program called *Window On Wallstreet*:

> It's a fact. Today's markets move fast. Very fast. Too fast to rely on end-of-day or delayed data feeds. To stay competitive you need up-to-the-minute information at your fingertips. Quotes ticking in. News breaking through as it happens. And charts instantaneously updating. You need streaming, real-time data.

No, you don't. The long-term investor, you'll recall, does not need split-second information. Real-time quotes and charts are distractions, not advantages. Most do-it-yourselfers should be in it for the long haul, not for the next hour.

Using eSignal, a popular service from Data Broadcasting

Corp., you would see on your computer screen a list of real-time quotes with upticks in green and downticks in red. Another window would show your portfolio, again in real time so that you can see how much money you made or lost in the past thirty seconds. At the bottom of your screen is a window that scrolls news headlines as they are released on the wires. At the top of your screen is a running ticker tape showing symbols and their latest trades. Using eSignal, you can specify alert prices for any stock and be notified by e-mail, pager, mobile phone, or all three. The example given in the eSignal demo shows alerts placed on Microsoft at 80 and 82 with the stock currently trading for 83.

Now, there's a relaxed day. Picture this: You're a mother driving your children to swimming lessons when out of the blue comes a phone call. "Microsoft trading at 82," says a computer voice. You screech to the side of the road, children held in place by their seatbelts. You push the speed dial button to your broker and immediately sell half your position. "Okay, kids," you say brightly, convinced that you saved the family jewels. "Off we go." Three blocks later, the phone rings again. "Microsoft trading at 80." Screech! Speed dial, sell the remaining shares of Microsoft. "Mommy, what's wrong?" asks one child. "Nothing, I'm just trading stocks. Ready for your swimming lesson?"

I wouldn't be at all surprised if the price of Microsoft then rebounded back up to 90 and higher in later weeks. The amazing technology of the computer is a wonderful way to scare yourself out of a good thing. Yet, the most popular software packages continue to market themselves to people who seem to crave that kind of split-second timing. A February 2000 ad for OmniTrader supplied this quote from satisfied customer Peter Grymkoski:

> I used to make about 6 trades a year, with very little success. I have made 54 trades using OmniTrader, and my percent of return is 16.49 percent—annualized it is 391.03 percent. Even when the markets were down, OmniTrader has identified successful buy candidates for me. Each and every week has been profitable. The success I have had with OmniTrader has me so overwhelmed that I can hardly sleep at night, just waiting for the next market day to open!

That's my dream come true—sleepless nights spent anticipating the opening bell so I can start frantically trading. Mr. Grymkoski looks back with sadness at the days when he would suffer through an entire year with only six trades. Now, thanks to OmniTrader, he's popping like corn in hot oil, and life is good.

Most of the successful do-it-yourself investors I know would be thrilled to go an entire year with only six trades, or no trades for that matter. They would not be aware of Microsoft dropping from 83 to 82 to 80 in the course of a day. They might read at the end of a month that Microsoft has reached its lowest stock price in six months, and decide to buy a few more shares. Even if they had decided to start selling Microsoft at 82, many would have done so with a limit order, not an automatic price alert that triggers a phone call and a market order.

> **Limit order:** a type of stock order where you specify your price to buy or sell and then leave the order on the books for the day or until canceled. You don't need to watch the market anymore because the order will automatically execute if the stock reaches your price. In this case, the order would have sold Microsoft at 82. You'll read more about order types in "The Art of the Order" on page 95.

In general, avoid frenzy. Software tends to create frenzy. More information is not always better—I don't care what eSignal's slogan wants you to believe. Its website reads, "You'll make more, because you'll know more." Make more *what*? Mistakes?

There is a segment of the individual investment population that loves to trade, and for them such software is a tonic. I'm sure some of those people do indeed achieve spectacular results, as Mr. Grymkoski claims to have done. However, the great majority of do-it-yourself investors will never daytrade. The great majority of those who do will lose money. They try their hand at stock market speculation with tools like eSignal, MetaStock, OmniTrader, TeleChart, Telescan, TradeStation, and Window On Wallstreet. When all is said and done, trading costs a lot of money and results in poor performance for most people. And remember this: The natural response to an outlay of cash for trading software is to expect it to produce results. That's the old "It will pay for itself in the long run" rationale. That's a no-win proposition and another reason to avoid trading software. Remember that $2,000 set of golf clubs, the $300 tennis racket, or the $150 pair of running shoes? They didn't really improve the quality of your game, did they?

Which puts us back at square one in trying to harness your computer for investment success. If it doesn't come from frequent trading, is there any hope for effectively using your computer?

The Saving Grace of a Database

Yes, there's an effective way to use your computer for investing. Stock databases that help you find companies matching a set of criteria that you consider important can reduce your research time. You can search for companies with low price-to-earnings, low price-to-sales, high cash flow, and high profit margin. You can find companies that are growing fast, previous high-fliers that are now way down in price, and all the competitors facing a company that you're considering. Nearly every stock measurement is a searchable criterion in a database program.

That's a lot of power, but even then you might be surprised at its limited usefulness. You could end up paying $300 for the software plus a monthly subscription to the data and spend hours combing through the database only to find the very same stocks covered in this month's issue of *SmartMoney*.

While I often sneer at the results achieved by professional investors, I will concede here my envy of fully staffed research departments. Teams at Fidelity, Janus, Goldman Sachs, Standard & Poor's, Morningstar, and others do nothing but search the world for attractive investments. The odds are good that by the time you search your stock database and find a good company, others already know about it. The media are all over the people on those research teams, hunting for tips to print, broadcast, or upload. That's why you will so often find your "discoveries" on the cover of *SmartMoney*. That fact has not kept people from using two popular databases: Morningstar Principia Pro for Stocks and Power Investor. The former offers data on 8,000 stocks for $95 per year while the latter covers 11,000 for $92 per year.

Robert Franklin of San Francisco has used Power Investor extensively and loves it. "I find Power Investor to be much better than the Internet. It's faster, puts everything in one place, and has better searching and ranking tools. Whenever I hear of a company to buy, I write down its name and check it in Power Investor when I get home. If it looks good, I'll click a button to see the company's competitors. You wouldn't believe the number of times this simple second step has led me to great companies. I remember when a friend mentioned that Compaq was his favorite computer company and that he was buying shares of the stock. He wanted me to do the same, so I checked out Compaq in Power Investor. A quick look at the competitor's screen revealed Dell and Gateway. I ended up buying those instead and outperforming my friend." There are certainly noncomputer methods available to discover a company's competitors, but Robert illustrates well the value of a good stock database as a complement to your focused reading and always alert mind.

For mutual funds, there are again two databases that I repeatedly encounter: Morningstar Principia Pro for Mutual Funds and Steele Mutual Fund Expert. The former offers data on 10,000 funds for $295 per year of quarterly updates, while the latter covers 12,000 for $107 per year of quarterly updates. "Mutual Fund Expert and a monthly newsletter comprise the only research I do," says Martin French of Uvalde, Texas. "I decided years ago that I don't feel comfortable owning individual stocks, so I put everything in mutual funds. But I like to be aggressive. I choose sector funds and single-country funds, and I concentrate my money in just a few. Expert lets me create my portfolio to watch and lists of funds that compete with my current holdings. That lets me see instantly whether I'm in the best of breed or something else. I don't switch willy-nilly because I understand that performance fluctuates. But if I put a category of funds on a comparison chart—something that's a cinch with Expert—and I see a consistent monthly underperformance in my fund, I'll move to the consistent winner."

I use both Power Investor and Mutual Fund Expert and my experience echoes the testimonials of Robert and Martin. The programs provide as much hands-on research as you need without overwhelming you with information the way trading software does. Plus, with contact info for every investment such as phone, mailing address, and web address, the software makes it simple for you to continue your research along traditional paths. Each fund in Expert even displays a button that you click to go immediately to the fund's website. It doesn't get much simpler than that.

> Mutual Fund Expert
> Power Investor

To recap, you should steer clear of trading software because you have a life to live outside of your investment portfolio and should therefore focus on long-term results. That means you don't need real-time information or price alerts. Instead, you should use stock and fund databases to complement your alert mind and traditional research. Even then, you will often see that professionals have already found and revealed your discoveries. Which leads conveniently into the next section.

Copy Successful Professionals

The best benefit of absorbing everything for a while is that you come to know what kind of information is available. As you hone your investment strategy into a plan that fits your schedule and temperament, you'll probably develop a few tricks to help you get ahead.

One of the most common tricks among do-it-yourselfers is copying successful pros. It may not be the most heroic way to get ahead, but it does seem to work. It's also an interesting twist on the do-it-yourself theme. Instead of relying only on your own efforts, you piggyback on professionals for free advice, then put that advice to work on your own. Given the wide availability of free professional advice, it's a mystery to me why some people continue paying for it. Investment magazines and newspapers often print the latest picks from newsletter writers, analysts, and fund managers. Such people also provide comments on radio and television from time to time. Immediately acting on their advice with abandon isn't the smartest approach to take, but listening to them and following up on a few good ideas with research of your own is smart.

Catching professionals on radio and TV programs is a hit-or-miss proposition. You don't know who the guests will be, whether they're any good, or if you'll be able to see or hear the program. Besides, given the media's high ratio of worthless info to useful info, the odds of getting anything helpful are against you. A more reliable way to tap the minds of professionals you admire is to choose your favorite mutual fund managers. You can call anytime to request their latest quarterly report. It will show you exactly where the fund manager has invested in recent months. These reports are not always timely, so you might be viewing the fund's holdings as of six months ago. Still, the list of investments is a great starting point for picking your own stocks. You can either research the names on the list and see if they appear attractive to you, or use the names to get an idea for the right industries to research. Either way, you've saved yourself a lot of open-market research time.

If you like a manager enough, you can always invest your money in the fund. You'll not only benefit from the performance of the fund, you'll also automatically receive reports detailing the holdings. I've used this strategy for years with Ron Baron, manager of Baron Asset Fund. His reports are written in a lively manner and can help you pick out winners. Those reading Baron's letters in 1995 might have decided to buy shares of Charles Schwab & Company, the discount brokerage firm. Split adjusted, you could have bought shares for around $1.70 in January 1995. They traded at $29 in January 2000. Not bad money for just reading a letter.

Investor's Business Daily takes this concept one better each Friday. In its "Funds & Personal Finance" section, the paper runs various features analyzing the buys and sells of mutual fund families and institutional money managers. One of my favorites is called "New Buys of Top-Rated Funds." The table is limited to purchases of mutual funds rated A− or higher, which equates to those placing in the top 15 percent of all funds in three-year performance. *IBD* sorts the companies in the table by their relative price strength and earnings per share ratings; stocks with the best stock price performance and fastest earnings growth are listed first. The table also shows how many top-rated funds bought the stock in the latest reporting period. If you're thinking of a stock but aren't quite sure about it, seeing it on this list means that it has passed muster with leading money managers and analysts. That will give your confidence a boost.

The October 1999 list was topped by market leaders such as Qualcomm, Applied Micro Circuits, Siebel Systems, JDS Uniphase, and Clarify. From the October listing to market close on February 10, 2000, the companies posted respective returns of 169 percent, 248 percent, 135 percent, 217 percent, and 258 percent. The top fifteen names on the list rose an average of 114 percent. Extending the time period, in the twenty months from October 1999 to June 2001, Qualcomm gained 32 percent and Siebel Systems gained 176 percent. JDS Uniphase, however, lost 41 percent. Still, not bad.

Is this another version of The Winning System? No. The March 2000 list was topped by Emulex, Infosys, and i2 Technologies. In the next two months, the three stocks dropped 76 percent, 52 percent, and 42 percent respectively. By June 2001 they were down 64 percent, 80 percent, and 75 percent. Those were bad times in the market and the pros didn't fare any better than the rest of us.

By the way, if you want to see what the funds are selling, *IBD* has you covered there as well. It prints a table called "New Sells of Top-Rated Funds." The top ten stocks on that list in October 1999 lost an average of 12 percent by February 2000. That's impressive considering that the Nasdaq gained 58 percent during the same time period.

Do-It-Yourself Investor Tools

From your placid home office, you'll need to conduct investment research. You'll welcome a limited amount of information from sources you've come to like and ignore everything else.

Chapter Recap

Here's a rundown of what you learned in this chapter.

- **Think Like an Investor:** The first step to effective research is thinking like an investor, a person who makes money with the money they already have. You'll watch the world around you for opportunities to profit. Vacations are a time to relax and enjoy yourself, but they're also a chance to see profits where you don't normally look. As a person who thinks like an investor, you will go through life paying attention, drawing conclusions, and acting on those conclusions. Put your money to work. As Ben Franklin pointed out, "Money makes money, and the money money makes makes more money."

- **Absorb Everything:** When you're first starting out, absorb everything. You don't know what's good and what's bad, so don't try to discern yet. Read every business and investment publication you can get your hands on. Hang out in the library with a notepad and pen. Watch the financial TV programs and listen to the radio money shows. Absorb, absorb, absorb. One day, you'll find yourself already aware of most of what you encounter. Then you're ready for the next step.

- **Focus Your Research:** After a time, you'll tire of absorbing everything and decide to focus on just the good stuff. You'll know which publications appeal to you and fit your budget. You will be pleased to discover that many ordinary sources like your daily newspaper and magazines available at the grocery store compete well with professional reports costing hundreds of dollars. There's a balance you'll achieve where you know just enough to keep your money humming upward, but not so much that you're confused.

- **Learn What to Ignore:** In your evolution as a keen researcher, you'll progress from absorbing all information to carefully selecting information to being able to filter the selected information. What you choose to filter out is a personal choice: some investors ignore economic data released by Washington; others ignore daily price movements of their holdings; a few ignore overall market behavior. Half of being smart is knowing what you're dumb at. Likewise, half of being an informed investor is knowing which information you don't need.

- **Use Investment Software the Smart Way:** Too often, investment software is considered a tool for daytrading, as evidenced by the fact that so much investment software is marketed as the best way to stay up-to-the-minute. You don't need that. If anything, you need software that simply helps you find investments that meet your criteria. Even then you'll be surprised at how many times your "discoveries" are already discussed in the magazines you read. Still, there's power in the computer and many investors consider a good database to be an excellent complement to their traditional research.

- **Copy Successful Professionals:** A shortcut that helps a lot of individual investors and can help you is to copy successful professionals. Mutual fund managers, analysts, and newsletter editors spend every day scouring the market for good ideas. While you're at work or with your family or reading in the park, teams of suits are crunching numbers for profit—you might as well see what they're finding. One good way to do so is by reading the reports sent out by your favorite mutual fund managers. They show the fund's holdings from a recent period and will probably give you some good leads. Another good technique is to read *Investor's Business Daily* on Fridays, when it prints stocks that top-rated mutual funds are buying and selling.

Resources from This Chapter

From the many tools available to you, several emerge as the best. Each has my own stamp of approval. Everything listed here has been helpful to me.

Newspapers

Surprise, surprise, there's only one daily paper that you should consider.

- **Investor's Business Daily** is without a doubt the best investment newspaper. Just look at the name! Everything in the paper is investment oriented, even the news stories. The front page contains "IBD's Top Ten" news items in brief, the backside of the front page condenses dozens of additional stories in a feature called "To the Point." Inside you'll find interviews with leading fund managers and analysts, price charts for companies in the news, and stock screens and fund screens that use *IBD*'s proprietary Smart-Select Corporate Ratings with the legendary EPS and RPS ranks. If you're going to subscribe to a daily paper, this is the one. Annual subscriptions cost $197. You can also buy individual issues of *IBD* off the newsstand for $1. (800) 831-2525; <u>www.investors.com</u>

Magazines

Monthly magazines should form the heart of your regular reading. They provide a good look at the big picture, and reading them is the least you should do to keep on top of what's happening.

- **SmartMoney** is the "*Wall Street Journal* Magazine of Personal Business" and does a better job with investment information than the venerable journal itself. Sporting much of the best financial writing, incisive research, and refreshing accountability, *SmartMoney* will help any individual reach the top of the performance charts. I have subscribed for years and consider regular reading to be a basic investment requirement. Annual subscriptions cost $24. (800) 444-4204; <u>www.smartmoney.com</u>

- **Worth** is slightly more intellectual than *SmartMoney*, occasionally running ten-page articles on single companies or the prospects of a developing country. I enjoy the detail. The list of columnists reads like a who's who of the investment world: Peter Lynch, Walter Russell Mead, Robert X. Cringely, Jim Rogers, and Andrew Tobias among others. The magazine shows what top fund managers are buying now, what newsletter editors are recommending, and what expert analysts suggest buying and selling from the stocks in their sector. You won't waste a minute reading *Worth*. Annual subscriptions cost $24. (800) 777-1851; <u>www.worth.com</u>

Internet

While many successful investors still do not use the Internet, it's tough to overlook its usefulness. There's a lot of garbage, however, so I've narrowed the list of destinations to a short one, far shorter than the occasional "best of the web" collections you'll see on newsstands. For quick links to each resource below, visit my site at **www.jasonkelly.com/doityourself.html**.

- **Bigcharts** is the best place to get free investment charts. They're customizable by time frame, benchmarks displayed for comparison, and chart style. You can even click to get a printer-friendly version of the chart. While other sites like Yahoo Finance show basic price charts, you'll want to stop by Bigcharts for a deluxe view of past performance. **www.bigcharts.com**

- **CBS MarketWatch,** billing itself as "Your Eye on the Market," provides an alternative to *SmartMoney*. It collects the latest news headlines, naturally, but also brings top columnists who offer you their take on developments. Thom Calandra writes about technology, economist Irwin Kellner comments on the big picture with lots of musings about the Federal Reserve, and Paul Erdman provides his two cents on just about everything. **cbs.marketwatch.com**

- **ClearStation** calls itself "The Intelligent Investment Community." Members provide their own picks and pans from the market, and the site tracks their performance. You can see who's done well, what their current portfolio looks like, and follow along for whatever profit or loss they achieve. It's free to register, after which you'll be an official "clearhead." You can also elect to receive daily stock ideas from the A-list of amateur analysts. ClearStation is a great way to find potential investments, but be sure to conduct your own research before following any advice. At the very least plug in the stock symbol at Yahoo Finance and find out what the company does to make a buck. **www.clearstation.com**

- **iExchange** is similar to ClearStation. Every individual here is called an analyst, and everybody's performance is tracked. The best among the group bubble to the top and are revealed on the home page. Visitors to the site can purchase reports from winning analysts and follow along with their strategies. The performances are impressive, and you can have the site search for the top analysts defined by several factors like predictive accuracy or annualized return. Here again, do your own research before you make a decision. www.iexchange.com

- **JasonKelly.com** is a handy resource for my readers. You'll find updates to information contained in my books, articles on current investment issues, tips for retirement, and other financial pointers. I keep the most important research links on the top page in a box called "Kelly's Command Center." The links don't just take you to the top page of the destination, they take you directly to where you want to go. For instance, the "Historical Quotes" link goes to the page at Yahoo Finance where you input a ticker symbol and time period to get the opening, high, low, and closing price for each day during the period. If nothing else, come to JasonKelly.com to get yourself on my free e-mail list. I promise not to send you any credit card ads. www.jasonkelly.com

- **Morningstar** has been the definitive source of mutual fund information for years and has diversified its coverage to include stocks. That dual focus, combined with the company's expertise in presenting research, has produced a superb investment website. The usual discussion boards and portfolio tracking are in place, along with features that you won't find elsewhere, such as "ClearFuture," the site's step-by-step retirement planner. You'll be surprised at how much of Morningstar's premium research is available on the website for free. www.morningstar.com

- **The Motley Fool** is one of the most popular investment sites online. The Fools hate mutual funds and love small company stocks. They track real portfolios with superb reports on each stock owned. The site's claim to fame is its extensive message board system covering almost every public company. The level of thought that goes into many of the posts is enlightening, far above what I've run into elsewhere online. If you're wondering about a stock, swing by The Motley Fool and see what its community thinks. Typing the symbol will take you straight to a discussion about your stock, or you can view the top 25 boards for new investment ideas. **www.fool.com**

- **Multex** is the place to go for professional analyst reports. Many of them are free; others cost anywhere from $5 to $150. "The Analyst Corner" features subscriber questions answered by pros. You probably won't need to pay for professional analysis after taking full advantage of all the free resources listed here. But if you ever do, now you know where to find it. **www.multex.com**

- **Raging Bull** is another solid message board site. The tone is more irreverent than that of The Motley Fool, but not offensive. Tech stocks are the focus, and many of the posters are engineers, marketers, or other folks with inside knowledge that they're dying to share. If you want a place brimming with smart people fishing for the stock of the year, you just found it. **www.ragingbull.com**

- **SmartMoney** maintains a dynamite investment site. With unique Java tools like a map of the market and a tear-off portfolio watchlist, it's a wonder this site doesn't charge money. (It's possible that it will soon, but for now it's free.) The same top-flight journalists who write for the magazine contribute articles to the site, all archived for easy retrieval. Among my favorite features are the pundit watch, which tracks the calls of top Wall Street analysts, and the updates on how *SmartMoney* recommendations are performing. If a good company dips, you'll see it here and can consider buying on sale. **www.smartmoney.com**

- **TheStreet.com** founder James J. Cramer once called his site, "The Motley Fool with a brain." As a fan of The Motley Fool, I find that to be a harsh way to put it, but I will tip my hat to TheStreet.com. It provides more daily articles from pros than any other site I've visited. There are tech articles and healthcare articles, tips on charting and tips on reading a company's fundamentals. **www.thestreet.com**

- **Worldlyinvestor** specializes in—you guessed it—global investing. Its columnists write largely about foreign markets, but you'll also find domestic information covered with aplomb. Among my favorite contributors are Paul Merriman on mutual funds, Barbara Rockefeller on technology, Stefan Spath on Latin America, and Nadine Wong on biotech stocks. At the time of this writing, Worldlyinvestor offered three daily e-mail newsletters and seventeen weeklies with titles like *Morning Financial Update, Stocks to Watch, Internet Stocks*, and *Asia Stocks*. **www.worldlyinvestor.com**

- **Yahoo Finance** is the champion investment site. It aggregates most of what you will ever need to know about a stock or mutual fund into one free location. Company and fund profiles are complete with management information, contact numbers, price history, split history, recent announcements—and everything else you'd expect. Profit margin? It's there. Return on investment? It's there. From how the company did in the last five years to how it did in the last hour, Yahoo Finance has you covered. You can create as many portfolios and watch lists as you want. Everything is fast and free. **finance.yahoo.com**

Newsletters

Investment newsletters aren't necessary to your success, but they can be helpful and one good recommendation will pay for the subscription price. Most newsletters will be happy to send you a sample for review.

- **The Chartist** looks for stocks based on technical analysis. It seeks stocks with the highest relative strength, that is, the ones that have performed better than the averages and should continue doing so. The newsletter's actual cash account has been published since 1969 and has averaged more than 18 percent for the past ten years. Annual subscriptions cost $175. (800) 942-4278.

- **Morningstar FundInvestor** and **StockInvestor** bring information from one of the leading investment research shops. *FundInvestor* delivers 44 pages of articles, full-page fund profiles, interviews, and coverage of 500 selected mutual funds. *StockInvestor* delivers 32 pages of fundamental information on companies rather than stock tips. It also covers 500 stocks divided up like this: 300 undervalued companies, 150 blue chips and other popular stocks, and 50 microcaps that Morningstar deems the most attractive. Annual subscriptions cost $99 for *FundInvestor* and $149 for *StockInvestor*. (800) 735-0700; **www.morningstar.com**

- **MPT Review** is Louis Navellier's high-performance monthly. He uses quantitative analysis to crunch the numbers and come up with a list of high-return, low-risk stocks. Then he looks closer at each company to find the few with fat profit margins and earnings growth. He arranges that final list into conservative, moderate, and aggressive portfolios. Annual subscriptions cost $275. (800) 454-1395; **www.mptreview.com**

- **The NeatSheet** is my monthly stock and mutual fund letter. It follows the research guidelines set forth in my *Neatest Little Guide* series of books to assemble "Kelly's Quicklist" of the best funds and stocks. This two-page spread covers nearly all the numbers you'd want to know. I assemble those winners into nine fund portfolios on a grid that ranges from short-term with little money to long-term with lots of money, so, no matter where you are in your investment career, there's a portfolio for you. There are also two stock portfolios, one for the general market and one for higher-risk stocks. I write the three-page article myself every month, which is why the price is so cheap. Annual subscriptions cost $75. (800) 339-5671; **www.jasonkelly.com**

- **No-Load Fund Investor** has been covering mutual funds longer than most funds have been in existence. Its editor, Sheldon Jacobs, is one of the best-known newsletter editors, appearing often at conferences and providing quotes to the media. The newsletter covers nearly a thousand no-load funds and prints articles on the latest news and strategies. There are model portfolios for conservative, moderate, and aggressive investors. Annual subscriptions cost $139. (800) 252-2042; **www.sheldonjacobs.com**

- **The Outlook** is published weekly by Standard & Poor's. It's one of the most widely read investment newsletters, appearing at the reference desk of most public libraries in a three-ring binder. Analysts write about their favorite ones and show which ones meet their various filters like the Short-Term Appreciation Ranking System (STARS), Fair Value Portfolio, and Platinum Portfolio. Annual subscriptions cost $298. (800) 852-1641.

- **The Value Line Investment Survey** is published weekly by Value Line. This is no breezy read on the walk back from the mailbox. Each installment is a booklet of one-page data sheets on 135 or so stocks. The data sheets are a study in efficiency. Rarely is so much information packed into a space so small. There's a chart, a table with historical info like cash flow per share and average annual P/E ratio, insider buys and sells, and commentary from one of Value Line's analysts. After thirteen weeks of saving the booklets, you have a binder covering 1,700 stocks in more than 90 industries. Then the cycle repeats and you begin replacing each thirteen-week-old booklet with the newest edition. It's slick. *The Neatest Little Guide to Stock Market Investing* contains an in-depth look at how to get the most out of *Value Line*. It even includes a sample *Value Line* page with various sections numbered and explained. Annual subscriptions cost $570. (800) 833-0046; **www.valueline.com**

Software

Good research software on your computer doesn't change the tenets of good investing, but it can save lots of time and possibly lead you to investments you would not have otherwise discovered. Stick with research programs, not trading programs.

- **Mutual Fund Expert** is the software I use to find top mutual funds. It covers more than 12,000 funds with a system that's easy to use. You can group funds, build portfolios, search by anything, sort by anything, and graph however you want. Annual subscriptions cost $221 for monthly updates and $107 for quarterly updates. (800) 237-8400; **www.mutualfundexpert.com**

- **Power Investor** is published by the Investors Alliance. It covers 11,000 stocks in a system that allows you to find, filter, sort, group, and graph to your heart's content. It's a lot faster than the Internet, and your various groupings are always saved right on your hard drive. I use Power Investor regularly and write commentary about it on my website, **www.jasonkelly.com**. I suggest reading the information at my site before you buy. Annual subscriptions cost $92 for daily downloads. (800) 477-7188; **www.powerinvestor.com**

5 / The Path to the Simplest Investment Plan Ever

This chapter is about the brass tacks of do-it-yourself investing: brokers, orders, a few techniques that have helped others, and an unveiling of the simplest investment plan ever.

Let's start by finding the right broker and placing the right orders. Then we'll see that it's better to find a few good investments than a large mixed bag. Next we'll consider the wisdom of sticking it out through good times and bad. It doesn't just apply to marriage anymore. Then we'll wade—not dive—into the world of investing. Safer on the head, you see, and on your assets too. Finally, and with great fanfare, I will reveal the simplest investment plan ever.

We begin with a drive down the Golden State Freeway.

Brother-in-Law Brokers

Researching an article I was writing on full-service brokers, I took a drive down the Golden State Freeway to meet Nancy Navarro, president of an investment club in Carlsbad, California. I'd read that her club was designed for novice investors and that most of the newcomers had accounts with full-service brokers. Nancy's mission was to wean the neophytes from that expensive, misleading bottle. "Most folks think a broker can coach them through the bad times," Nancy said. "They expect the broker to call and tell them everything's going to be all right. Boy are they surprised when the tough times come and their broker calls wanting to sell. You don't get much from a broker anymore. They don't have access to any information you can't get yourself. They don't know any more about the markets than you can learn with a little reading. They face the same emotions you face. They're just like you, but they charge."

There was a time when investors relied on end-of-day stock prices in the newspaper and mailings from potential companies. That was as timely as individual research got. People back then relied on their brokers to keep them in the know. Not anymore. Today, anybody can see the latest news as quickly as the media reports it and usually faster than a typical broker. You can read SEC filings straight from the source, listen to conference calls directly or read their transcripts, and see real-time price quotes. Not that you'll need them much if you invest for the long term, but they're available.

"Most people joining my club are nervous at first," Nancy told me. "That's why they opened accounts with full service brokers. They wanted hand-holding because they'd been told that investing is too difficult for the average person to do on their own. Now that they've been in the club for a while and had a chance to see ordinary folks just like themselves making good investment decisions, they don't want to pay full-service prices anymore."

Ever Hear of a Company Called Intel?

What the full-service brokerage industry is loathe to admit is that their brokers were never about objective advice. They have always been an in-house sales staff posing as financial advisors.

A friend of mine swears by his stockbroker, but also swears that his allegiance has nothing to do with the fact that his stockbroker is his brother-in-law. "He calls with great recommendations," my friend said.

"And how does he find those recommendations?" I asked.

"By researching the markets. Long hours of research."

Right. I gave the brother-in-law broker a call, posing as a journalist doing a story on the benefits of full-service investment banking for individuals. He never suspected a thing.

"So," I began, "I'm told that you've come up with some

great investment ideas over the years." He agreed with me. "How important would you say the investment banking division of your company has been to your success?"

"Well, I get my ideas from the research division. They write up the reports and distribute them to the brokerage staff."

"Most of the research is done by them?"

"That's right."

"Do they scour the markets for the ideas they generate?"

"What do you mean? What else would they scour?"

"Beats me. Are you as likely to see research reports on, say, a tiny company in Iowa that you've never heard of as you are to see reports on a multinational that your investment banking division represents?"

"Oh, the list of companies we usually see is a very select list. A tiny company in Iowa might make it if it meets the criteria, but that rarely happens."

"What are the criteria?"

"It has to be of high-enough quality to make our investment banking division's cut. If not, the research department won't bother with it, and I won't ever see a report on it."

"That means the company needs to be represented by your investment banking division."

"Not necessarily." His voice had changed slightly.

"Not officially, but have you ever seen a research report from your firm on a company that it didn't represent?"

"Well, I see so many reports, I can't remember which ones were authored in house or not. It's hard to say."

"Do you have any reports handy now?"

"You mean as we talk?"

"Yes, right there in front of you on the desk. You say there are so many reports that you can't remember all the sources. Then there must be a few on your desk today."

"Yeah, here's one from our firm about one of our companies. Here's another." I heard the sound of shuffling papers in the background, followed by a puff of exhaled air across the receiver. "Well, today all I have are in-house reports."

"Any of them covering outside companies?"

"Not today."

"Do they ever?"

"Like I said, I can't recall all the reports."

This is circumstantial evidence, to be sure, but let's recap what the brother-in-law broker revealed. That stock he's recommending to my friend on the phone isn't something he dug up after hours spent searching through SEC filings, earnings projections, and industry reports. It's what the research division of the investment bank wrote up the night before. So the research division did the research, right? Not exactly. They were simply told by the investment banking division to push the stock, which is one that the company represented in its initial public offering and continues to shephard in the marketplace—a service for which it charges handsomely.

> *Initial public offering:* Abbreviated IPO, this is a company's first sale of stock to the general public. To "go public," a company works with the investment banking side of a large brokerage firm like Goldman Sachs, Merrill Lynch, or Paine Webber. Such firms want the companies they represent to do well, hence they instruct their research division to analyze the stocks in a positive light so the retail division will sell the shares to clients.

Full-service brokers often tell you about a stock you would never otherwise have considered or about one that is such an obvious choice that you're laughing at the so-called research that went into it.

One of Nancy's club members received an urgent call from her broker telling her to buy a hot technology company.

"What's it called?" she asked.

"Intel. They make microprocessors, the chips in computers. Computers are becoming very popular."

This might have been astute if it had happened in the '80s, but it was *1997*. Like she'd never heard of Intel before. Like she hadn't noticed that computers were popular. This is research?

How to Save $792 per Order

The money people save by switching to online discount firms from full-service brokers is astounding. A May 2000 study by *Technology Investor* found that online trading shaves up to

99 percent off the full-service price. That's the difference between paying $800 to buy a stock and paying only $8. The $792 savings is a decent investment all by itself when grown at 11 percent. In ten years it would be worth $2,250. Imagine the change in your fortune if you invested a $792 commission savings four times per year. In ten years at 11 percent that plan would produce more than $56,000—all from your commission savings! What an effortless way to reduce your risk. You would have to make an awful lot of mistakes before you lost $56,000. Think of your commission savings as a type of financial safety net to reimburse you for the occasional investment gone wrong.

When you see the savings available online the question is not whether you should conduct your investments through an online discount broker but which of them to choose. I use Ameritrade for my stock portfolio. It charges a tiny $8 commission and executes trades quickly. The interface is slick, too, with real-time quotes available in a window at the bottom of every screen without leaving your current task. That means you can look at your portfolio while checking a price quote.

National Discount Brokers is another good choice. Its real-time portfolio screens let you see right away what your trades are doing to your portfolio. For newcomers, the site offers NDB University, with tutorials to get you up to speed. There's a checking account feature, credit cards, and even insurance. It costs $15 to trade stock, which is more than some of the others, but given the range of services it might be worth it.

For an even wider range of services, consider E*Trade, the best-known online broker. E*Trade executes trades quickly, and if you trade often enough, they give you faster quotes and other freebies. You can even book flights there and buy books. If it has to do with money, E*Trade has you covered. The one drawback I've found is that the site is heavily commercialized and slow. There's nothing that can tick you off faster than waiting to access your investment account while E*Trade loads an ad on your screen.

For mutual funds only, Fidelity and Schwab are excellent for their longstanding no-load, no transaction fee networks. Investing through these programs results in no commissions whatsoever.[*]

---

[*]That's assuming you don't switch around a lot. Both firms charge a commisision if you sell a fund within six months, but who cares? As a cool-headed investor, you shouldn't be doing that. It's a mutual fund, after all. Leave the buying and selling to the manager.

Both firms maintain physical branch locations where you can walk in and speak to a human being. Beware, though, that these two outstanding fund brokers are crummy stock brokers. Fidelity charges $25 while Schwab charges $30, exorbitant by online standards.

> ***No-load:*** means the mutual fund does not charge a commission to invest. In a true no-load fund, every penny of your investment goes into the fund.

Finally, I recommend Vanguard for index funds. An index mutual fund simply owns the stocks of a market index like the S&P 500, Wilshire 5000, or Nasdaq 100. There's no expensive team of researchers picking losing stocks, and there's very little trading. That keeps both costs and taxes low. The majority of U.S. stock funds return less than the S&P 500 over time and charge more than 1.25 percent per year to do so. Meanwhile, Vanguard's S&P 500 index fund always matches the performance of the S&P 500 and charges only 0.20 percent per year. It never outperforms, but it never underperforms either. You'll read on page 116 that the fund comprises my idea of "The Simplest Investment Plan Ever."

> **Ameritrade**
> **E*Trade**
> **Fidelity**
> **National Discount Brokers**
> **Schwab**
> **Vanguard**

Every broker I mentioned is insured through the Securities Investor Protection Corporation (SIPC) for up to $100,000 cash and $400,000 in other assets. SIPC is the same government-sponsored outfit that insures the expensive full-service brokers.

Opening a discount brokerage account is as easy as opening a bank account. Plus, all of these firms are good at transferring your existing full-service accounts. So what are you waiting for?

The Art of the Order

Having the right broker is a necessary step in the grand process of becoming a do-it-yourself investor, but hardly where the brass tacks hit bottom. Whether you place orders by walking into an office and sitting across the desk from a guy in a suit, by filling out a form and mailing it, by punching numbers on a telephone, or by clicking buttons on the Internet, the end result is the same. You buy or you sell. Your investment makes money or it loses money.

"I was taught to buy when I have the money," writes Mel Lewis of Kennesaw, Georgia. "I save until I have enough for 100 shares of whatever it is I'm buying, then I buy. If the price drops a bit before I have enough money, sometimes I get to buy sooner than expected. If it rises, I have to keep saving." Mel is describing market orders, which couldn't be simpler. When you want to buy, you buy. You pay the current price, end of discussion. If General Electric is trading at $150, Mel needs to save $15,000 to get his 100 shares.

Not everybody likes market orders. Take Warren Paulett of Cranston, Rhode Island. "Market orders are unnecessary," he says. "With a limit order, you can name your own price and nine times out of ten you get it. I save a few extra bucks on the buy, and I make a few extra on the sell." The limit order, so named because you set your own price limit, is a godsend to some investors and an unreliable source of stress to others. The former group, of which Warren is clearly a member, see a stock they like and decide what price to pay for it. Consider GE again. Instead of just paying $150 per share, the limit order crowd would enter an order to buy at $140, hoping for a quick downdraft to create the bargain price. If the downdraft comes the limit buyer picks up his 100 shares for $14,000, while Mel and the other market order buyers paid $15,000.

Chalk one up to the limit buyers. But of course it doesn't always go that way. You might miss your buy price by a point or two and then watch the stock double over the next few months. For want of a dollar or two you'll see some big ones get away.

A Stressful Argument About Stress Reduction

Both the market and the limit crowd stick to their order methods in the name of stress reduction. "It kills me to not know whether my order executed or not," Mel says. "You place a limit order that's good till canceled and weeks can go by with it just sitting there on the books. Did it go today? No, not today. Maybe it will tomorrow, maybe not. I can't stand that. I want a stock in my portfolio or out of my portfolio, not somewhere on deck."

> **Good till canceled:** Abbreviated GTC, this type of order stays on the books until you cancel it or it fills. It's not good forever, though. Most brokers get rid of the order after 60 days, at which point you can always place it again.

By contrast, Warren can't begin to understand Mel's difficulties. "That's the whole beauty of the limit order," he counters, "automating your entry and exit points. If anything, it's *more* certain because you spell out in the order what you're willing to pay on a buy or what you're willing to accept on a sell. Then you forget about it. You're not supposed to watch constantly after placing a good till canceled limit order. When it executes—if it ever does—you get an e-mail or a confirmation in your mailbox. You don't sweat the daily ups and downs; you just do your research once, decide what to pay for the stock, and live your life until it gets there. What could be less stressful?"

"What could be less stressful?" Mel repeats incredulously. "How about knowing that I've taken advantage of a price drop to lock in a good deal? The limit order leaves too much squishiness. A friend and I had been watching Dell Computer for months, waiting for a buying opportunity. In summer 1999 the stock dropped to the mid-30s. I waited a bit longer, then bought at $34 with a market order. My friend, thinking he was going to play it cool, put in a limit order to buy at $30. He was looking to pick up 300 shares, so the four-point savings meant $1,200, and he was already talking about what he could do with an extra $1,200. Guess what? The stock hit $31.38 on June 2, 1999, and never looked down again. Nine months later, it was trading at $55. I made 62 percent with a market order; he made nothing with a limit. Did I feel like a bozo when my $34 stock dropped to $32? No. I had researched Dell, knew it was a good company, and knew that $34 was a good price. A few bucks up and down don't matter in the long run. I say show your conviction with a market order."

What might help clear the air is to make a distinction in the kinds of stocks that work best with each order. Dell's price doesn't swing too wildly from day to day, so when it's down considerably that's usually after a steady deterioration. Some stocks, such as Internet and biotech, swing as much in twenty minutes as Dell swings all week. In that environment, a market order is far more uncertain than a limit order. (U P D A T E: Dell hit $16.25 in December 2000. The patient long-term user of limit orders could have picked it up for a song compared to Mel's Summer 1999 price of $34. Then again, maybe Mel had long ago sold that position in the 50s and used a market order to buy again at $18, while his friend put in a limit order to buy at $15. The benefits and drawbacks of each order type remain the same as prices change. One month after hitting $16.25, Dell traded at $26. That's a 60 percent gain in four weeks.)

What a Morning

I've experienced the sting of a fast-moving market myself when trying to make a few extra bucks off hot stock volatility. The pattern usually goes something like this. You're watching a stock for a while, waiting for the big breakout. Monday morning comes and it opens at $10, a full $3 above Friday's close. Then it goes to $12, $15, $18, $24, and *Holy Moly*, this is the big one!

Greed. Place that buy order at your online broker. In a separate browser window, start checking real-time quotes of the stock. Your order has been accepted, but you see after pressing the Refresh button half a dozen times that it hasn't executed yet. Or has it? Maybe the website just doesn't update as quickly as the market moves. You run the back of your hand across your forehead and lick your lips. The real-time quote window is not providing much help. The "big one" fizzled just seconds after you placed your buy. It went to $28, $23, $18, $13, $9, and *Holy Moly*, you sure hope your market order didn't kick in until later in the sequence.

Fear. After an eternity, the order shows up in the status window as having been filled at—you crack your knuckles—$27.50. A glance at the real-time quote screen shows the current price at $11. What a morning.

It's a rare bird who can look at that situation and describe it as a stress-free environment. A limit order at $15 would have been a true friend on that morning. Better yet, why not place a good till canceled limit at $5 and see what happens? Anything moving this much is not part of America's backbone, like GE or Ford Motor Company. It's a high flier and a dive bomber, and it might just dive into a $5 limit order one sunny morning in May. No watching required and none of that multiple-browser-window stress.

"I like limit orders for almost all of my purchases," Warren maintains. "Even for the big, slow-moving stocks. To me, most market stress comes from watching the market as it moves. I hate doing that, so I stopped a long time ago. Now, I look over my investments on Sunday and place any orders from the quiet of my den when there's no news breaking and no ticker tapes. I feel more in control that way. Four months ago I read a story about Fannie Mae in *Barron's* and saw that the stock was at $70. I checked my portfolio and decided I would allocate $5,000 to Fannie Mae, but I wanted 100 shares. That meant a limit buy at $50, which required a 29 percent drop from the current price. To the impulse buyer, it was crazy—who wants to wait around for that? Plus, what if it went to $150 in the meantime? Well, then I would have made a mistake. In this case, though, I was right. Fannie Mae did drop to less than $50 and like magic I had my 100 shares. I wasn't even watching it anymore. I read a few other stories about the company and saw that the price had dropped to $60 a couple months later, but I never changed my order. If I had put in a market order at $70, I'd be sitting on a 29 percent loss, waiting for a recovery. As it stands now, by the time the stock recovers I'll be sitting on a 40 percent gain, thanks to a limit order placed on a quiet Sunday."

An Art of Your Own

As you can see, there's no right way to handle your orders. There's an art to it, an art that is your own. Neither Mel nor Warren is a rash investor. One watches thoroughly researched stocks for the right time to buy, then buys at that time with a market order. The other determines after research the price he is willing to pay, sets that price in a limit order, then stops watching. Both approaches have been successful, and a combination isn't out of the question. You could use limit orders for volatile stocks and market orders for steady ones.

Win Few, Win Big

Shortly after becoming intrigued with my grandfather's investment skills, I decided that I wanted to be an investor too. I asked him what I should do to get started, and he told me to give him a $20 bill. Being only 11, I didn't have a $20 bill. He said that my lesson would have to wait until I did. Thinking that he was charging me for the lesson, I returned days later with the $20 and said I was ready to pay for my first investment class. He took my $20, put it in an envelope, and locked it in his desk drawer. That was the end of the class, he said. I would learn more the following week.

The week went by and I returned for my second class. He handed me the envelope, which I could tell by the thickness now contained more than just a single bill. I eagerly opened it and withdrew three bills, all $5s. "Grandpa, this is the wrong envelope," I told him. "Mine had twenty dollars in it."

"It's the same envelope," he answered. "This week, it's worth only fifteen dollars. What would you like to do?"

Take a different class, I thought. "I would like to get my twenty dollars back."

"Then come back next week."

The next week my envelope was down to just two $5 bills. "Grandpa, I thought you made money by investing. Why is my envelope losing money? Don't you have any other ones in your desk that I can use?"

His eyes lit up. "Yes, I do. Would you like to use one of those instead?" I nodded and he handed me a different envelope. I started to take my money out of the first envelope to transfer it into the new envelope when he said, "I sure hope the new envelope doesn't lose even more money." That made me pause. Instead of moving the money from the first envelope, I added the few dollars in my pocket to the new envelope and handed both back. My grandfather nearly jumped for joy. Feeling dejected and poor at the time, I didn't see why my grandfather was so happy. Now I do. He was thrilled to see his grandson not only discover the importance of diversifying investments but also opt not to take money out of a falling investment. He created an imperfect metaphor (if something had been wrong with my envelope, it would have been smarter to move the remaining $10 to a better one), but to an 11-year-old aspiring investor the lesson was clear: Don't put all your money in one envelope.

We're all aware of that lesson, usually presented in the more familiar form of "Don't put all your eggs in one basket." The problem I've discovered since stuffing envelopes at age 11 is that we take the wisdom of this lesson and overuse it. Putting all my money into one of my grandfather's envelopes was a bad plan. But it would have been just as bad to spread the money across every envelope in the drawer.

Accidentally Owning the Market

The terms used to describe getting your money to the right places are *asset allocation* and *diversification*. Asset allocation is dividing your money among different asset classes, such as large company stocks, small company stocks, bonds, cash, and so on. Asset classes were created to provide a big-picture look at the investment landscape so that you can know the general behavior of what it is you buy. For instance, a large company will probably behave differently than a small one. Some of your money should be invested in large companies and some in small so that your portfolio walks a steady path as each asset class rises and falls. Diversification takes the process one step further by suggesting that you own a variety of individual holdings instead of just one or two. Unfortunately, most financial publications extol the benefits of asset allocation and diversification without limits. They have taken what is a good idea—just like using several envelopes for your money is a good idea—and gone too far with it.

I attended an investment seminar in West Los Angeles recently to see what the competition was up to. The instructor told us that we should own lots of different stocks so that when one does poorly, the others can hold returns steady. I asked how many he meant by a lot, and he said at least fifty. That raised not only my eyebrows but also the volume in the room as people grumbled about the commissions involved in owning fifty stocks. I couldn't help noting that our instructor was a full-service broker, who would love nothing more than to see everybody own fifty stocks through his office. A man asked if mutual funds could achieve the diversification and simplify the process. The broker said no. Even with funds, he recommended owning at least twenty.

I would bet a drawer full of money-stuffed envelopes that a seminar like that one is being taught near you sometime this month. They're everywhere. And they're wrong. Say a typical mutual fund owns forty stocks, although many own far more than that. If you own twenty funds your portfolio consists of at least eight hundred stocks (discounting for stocks owned by more than one fund). You might as well buy an index fund at that point because your holdings are so widely distributed that you basically own the market. Actually, *more* than the market by some measures. The S&P 500 tracks only 500 stocks after all.

Diversification is smart because any one investment can burn out and leave you with nothing. But own too many investments and you'll suffer mediocre returns. "There was a time when I specifically set out to find small companies for my portfolio," writes Michael Coplin of Saco, Maine. "I read that small companies do better over time and figured I should add some of them to my portfolio. After that, I read that large companies have a distinct market advantage because of their greater spending power. They should form the core of a portfolio. I researched and bought several of them. Later I read that medium companies are actually the best things to own because they have much of the growth potential of the small companies but some of the spending power of the large. So I bought some of those. One day I glanced at positions on the monthly statement and was shocked to see that I owned twenty-eight stocks! I had to focus. One of those stocks was Home Depot, which has done marvelously well, but because it comprised less than 3 percent of my portfolio, it had little effect on my overall returns. I wish I'd had 50 percent in that stock." He bought Home Depot in 1995 for around $10 per share. Five years later it was trading at $65, a gain of 550 percent. But with only

3 percent of his money in Home Depot, Michael saw a boost to his overall portfolio performance of only 17 percent. That's nothing to sneeze at, but it's easy to see why he's shaking his head at not putting more on that stock.

Would putting 50 percent in Home Depot have been imprudent? In retrospect, no, but when you're buying stock you don't have the benefit of retrospect. Given the dearth of reliable crystal balls, yes, some people would consider it imprudent. But putting 8 or 10 percent into it would not have been. "The whole point of diversifying is to reduce risk," Michael continues, "but I've noticed when the market as a whole takes a dive, so do all my stocks. I'm not protected any better owning twenty-eight of them than I am owning fifteen of them."

The Safety of Twelve

Michael is correct. There are two kinds of risks with stock: business risk and market risk. Business risk is the chance that a company you own might hit the skids or go belly up. Intel might face higher chip prices from Asia and therefore lose profits. Loral might blow up its latest satellite model on the launchpad. Coke might make a few kids in Belgium sick. It's to protect against such business risks that you own more than one stock. Market risk has nothing to do with the saga of individual companies. It's the chance that the market as a whole will drop. Owning many companies won't do a darned thing to protect you against market risk because, when the market drops, they're all going with it. It's the same for mutual funds.

That being the case, the only risk you can hope to protect against is business risk, and it doesn't take fifty stocks to do it. In fact, statisticians crunched the numbers and came up with this revealing tidbit: 90 percent of business risk is eliminated by owning as few as twelve stocks. That's assuming they're not all in the same industry facing the same challenges, such as higher chip prices in Asia.

Actually, twelve stocks is a lot. What investor would not be proud to count among their holdings IBM, Home Depot, Wal-Mart, Boeing, Coca-Cola, American Express, J.P. Morgan, Merck, Starbucks, America Online, Disney, and Ford? It would take one heck of a problem to simultaneously destroy the businesses of all twelve companies. Their stock prices will fluctuate from day to day and would go down in a far-flung bear market, but their operations would remain intact. If some catastrophe was devastating enough to bankrupt all twelve of those companies, you'd have more to worry about than the value of your portfolio. Grab a shotgun and find a cave.

The Idiotic Frontier

You'll realize after trying to follow different asset classes that classifications aren't very helpful. When all you're deciding is how much to put into stocks and how much into the bank, that's a piece of cake. But when you're trying to figure out how much to put into small companies versus large, or tech companies versus healthcare, it gets trickier, and I don't see the benefit. It's the companies that matter. It seems to me you'd rather own a superb farming operation than a poorly run Internet shop. Just because the Internet company operates something new and exciting doesn't mean you need to own it.

The financial industry as a whole disagrees. It replaces that common sense with a love of efficiency so strong that it created a graph of risk and return called the *efficient frontier*. It supposedly reveals which classes of investments provide you with the most return for the risks you take. The idea is that you will create a perfect pie with stocks chosen in perfect proportion from the slices of market sectors. Four technology companies, six industrial giants, three healthcare outfits, five financial conglomerates, and so on.

What a waste of time. When you own too many stocks, you're taking a machine-gun approach when you should be sniping the best companies out there. If a machine-gun approach is what you want, then buy an index fund. Anytime you start owning a lot of stocks, go back and review the benefits of an index fund.

The grad school tidiness of the efficient frontier is so absurd that when you break it down it smacks of The Winning System. The class that's at the sweet spot of the efficient frontier changes over time. What is on top today won't necessarily be there tomorrow. Not long ago, technology was everybody's favorite. After 2000 it was everybody's hated stepchild. I bet it'll charm us again soon. Biotech comes in and out of fashion. Retail stores are usually snickered at, but not when technology implodes. Suddenly, selling real products to real people seems like a good idea. Even if you could accurately identify which sector of the market has the best prospects at any given time, what's to guarantee that you'll be able to choose the right company within that class? Nothing. Retail stores might be all the rage and you'll choose "Elmer's Trinket Emporium" as your hot stock. It goes from $35 to $3 while Dillard's, Target, and Wal-Mart rise 50 percent.

Which brings us back to the astute observation that it's better to own the best run company of the down-and-out class than the worst of the top class. If you ask me, that makes the whole idea of asset allocation as a good way to assemble a portfolio look pretty hazy.*

"If at First You Do Succeed, Quit Trying"

Shortly after you realize that dividing your portfolio by asset class doesn't work, you'll come to realize that diversifying too much is also a problem. The two go hand-in-hand because people trying to own a piece of all the right sectors have to pick a lot of stocks.

In case you think concentrating your portfolio is crazy, consider that Warren Buffett has held only three stocks at certain points in his investment career. In 1987, he invested 49 percent of his money in Capital Cities/ABC. If you find a great company and believe in it with all your heart, there's little safety in putting some of your money in a company that's not so great, just in case the great one stumbles. Great ones stumble, but they regain their stride. Buffett is a good expert to choose for this discussion, not only for his outstanding performance record but also for his firm belief in a focused portfolio. In his 1991 letter to Berkshire Hathaway shareholders, Buffett wrote:

> If my universe of business possibilities was limited, say, to private companies in Omaha, I would, first, try to assess the long-term economic characteristics of each business; second, assess the quality of the people in charge of running it; and, third, try to buy into a few of the best operations at a sensible price. I certainly would not wish to own

---

*It's opinions like this that keep me out of Manhattan's best cocktail parties.

an equal part of every business in town. Why, then, should Berkshire take a different tack when dealing with the larger universe of public companies? And since finding great businesses and outstanding managers is so difficult, why should we discard proven products? Our motto is: "If at first you do succeed, quit trying."

Perhaps our friend Michael should have paid attention to that motto when his Home Depot holding did well. He should have bought more Home Depot. He should have done it again the next year and the next. That approach can be traced back to an investor named Jesse Livermore, on whose trading career the book *Reminiscences of a Stock Operator* is based. He said that you pyramid your profits. When a stock does well, you add more to it. If it keeps doing well, you add more to it again. Commenting on Livermore's approach, *Investor's Business Daily* founder William O'Neil wrote in his book *How to Make Money in Stocks* that your objective in the market is not to be right but to make big money when you are right.

When picking stocks, stay focused. If you're going to own a little of everything anyway, do it in an index fund.

Keep Investing—The Advantage of Dollar-Cost Averaging

When your workweek has you down, buy more stock. If your hotwater heater breaks in February, send more money to your mutual fund. If there's one thing that can give you an edge over time, it's investing on a regular basis. "I send a monthly contribution to my portfolio no matter what's going on." That sums up the approach of Larry Wilson, an insurance agent in Conyers, Georgia. "When the headlines are terrible, it makes me feel good to know I'm benefiting from lower prices by purchasing more shares. When the headlines are good, it makes me feel good to be adding to my already successful account. There's just no better way to remain calm about the market than to send more money no matter what."

I agree, and Larry's approach is supported by the numbers. If you send in $500 a month to your favorite mutual fund or stock regardless of what it's doing, you'll end up paying less per share than the average price per share during the investment time period. It's called dollar-cost averaging.

How does this magic work? Your $500 buys more of the cheap shares and fewer of the expensive shares. Do that for a while and you'll have a whole raft of cheap shares and just a bucket of the expensive ones. Put the two sides on a balance and the overwhelming number of cheap shares tips your average buy price to the cheap side of things, just where you want it to be.

A Spoonful of Merck Every Month

Larry was buying shares of Merck from October 1999 to October 2000, at a rate of $500 per month. In October, the price was $79.50 and he bought 6.29 shares. By November, the price was down a bit to $78.50. He sent another $500, this time picking up 6.37 shares. In December, Merck was trading at $67.25, a loss of 15 percent from Larry's October purchase. "I didn't understand what was going on," he remembers. "Merck is a major pharmaceutical company, and the future of healthcare couldn't have been brighter as far as I could tell. I checked the financials at Yahoo and didn't see anything troubling, so I sent another $500." That bought a whopping 7.43 shares. Larry was then the proud owner of 20.09 shares of Merck.

The Year 2000 arrived and saw Larry's stock at $78.75 and him clicking his heels in the hallway. His December purchase gained 17 percent in just one month! He mentioned to his family at the breakfast table that it pays to stay true to your beliefs. "I told them I believed in Merck during its hour of darkness in December, and already I'd been rewarded. 'There's a lesson here, kids,' I declared." After breakfast, he sent another $500 to buy 6.35 shares.

In February the price was down to $61.75, the lowest Larry had seen. Breakfast was quieter but he was not harassed by the kids because they hadn't paid attention to him in January anyway. Nothing had changed at Merck, so he dutifully sent $500 to buy 8.10 shares. By March, the price was down to $57. He bought 8.77 shares with the final installment of his six-month experiment.

Here are the results of Larry's program:

KEEP INVESTING—THE ADVANTAGE OF DOLLAR-COST AVERAGING

Date	Investment	Price per Share	Shares Purchased
October	$500	$79.50	6.29
November	$500	$78.50	6.37
December	$500	$67.25	7.43
January	$500	$78.75	6.35
February	$500	$61.75	8.10
March	$500	$57.00	8.77
Totals	$3000	$70.46 (average)	43.31

Average Market Price per Share $70.46
Average Price Paid per Share $69.27
Average Savings per Share $1.19

Saving $1.19 per share might not seem like much, but it adds up over longer periods of time. The longer Larry keeps sending money on a regular basis, the more likely he is to buy shares at hugely different prices.

Also, despite the fact that Merck fell during this six-month period of Larry's investment program, sending money each month was the right thing to do. If instead he had invested the full $3000 in October at a price of $79.50, he would have owned only 37.74 shares and been sitting on a six-month loss of $849 in March. By buying steadily each month, he ended up owning 43.31 shares and incurred a loss of only $531 by March. That's a $318 savings achieved simply by sending the same amount of money each month regardless of Merck's price.

Raskob Revisited

Larry's approach works even in the worst of times. Remember John J. Raskob? I mentioned him on page 41 as an example of an expert financier who completely mistimed the market in 1929 by recommending that everybody invest $15 per month on margin. Anybody following that advice ended up broke from the Great Crash.

But there's an epilogue to Raskob's advice. Had he changed the part about investing on margin, he would have made a bunch of millionaires. Socking away $15 per month in Massachusetts Investors Trust from the Great Depression to now would have turned your account into more than $3 million. Granted, a 70-year time frame never hurts when trying to get ahead, but still you can appreciate the value of continuing to invest through thick and thin, good and bad, talkative breakfasts and quiet ones.

"I've always thought that if I'm not willing to buy more of a stock that has dropped a bit, then it must not be a very good company," Larry says. "Knowing that I own good companies is the best way to feel confident in every market condition. I think the folks running Merck know what they're doing. They're trying to make as much money as they can, and they're doing it in a good industry. If the price of their stock drops, I'm happy to buy more because the day will come when Merck is the talk of the town and I'll look like a genius. But I'm not a genius, I'm just persistent."

Wade In, Don't Dive

Larry's Merck experience illustrates a lot of things about this funny business of investing, not the least of which is that it's hard. If you can't trust a multibillion-dollar drug conglomerate to make you a few bucks, who can you trust? Some days you might get ahead with a few of your stocks, some days with none, and on a few days here and there you'll see everything rise together and kick yourself for not investing more. On margin, even. Whatever it takes to conquer the world.

Alan's April Massacre

Then comes a time—like the week of April 10, 2000—when the Nasdaq falls 25 percent, and Alan Abelson, the perennial bear at *Barron's*, giggles sardonically as he pens a column mocking all technology stock investors. With no sympathy for taxpayers still preparing their annual returns and counting on stocks for the money to send Uncle Sam, Alan wrote in his April 17, 2000, column:

> The mood in these parts seemingly overnight has gone from wild euphoria to profound funk. An investor's life has been transformed in a wink from a bowl of cherries to the pits.
>
> As you can imagine, it's a huge temptation for a grizzled and oft-baited bear like ourselves to revel in the carnage. And as we survey the wreckage, we can't help wondering which of the limbs sticking out from under the rubble belong to the momentum players, which to members of the buy-on-the-dip crowd, which to followers of the false prophets of Dow 36,000, and which to the other peddlers of New Era twaddle.
>
> But mother always told us not to be unseemly. Besides, nothing more unnerves us than the sound of weeping widows and wailing orphans. So we'll simply mention the fact that Nasdaq was down 25 percent for the week and 34 percent from its high, and the S&P 500 lost 10.5 percent, while the venerable Dow caved a whopping 805.71 points over the five trading sessions.

Still interested in the stock market? It pulls stunts like that now and then, every one of them chronicled by Alan's acerbic word processor. If one of the limbs sticking out from under the rubble of a recent tumble is yours, skip reading *Barron's* that weekend.

The damage was hard to ignore. Amazon.com sank to 58.5 percent off its high. Red Hat, the Linux operating system favorite, traded at $151 in December but by the end of the April Massacre was down to $24. If you think that's bad, your heart will bleed for CrayFish investors. That stock went from $166 in March to $13 in April, turning $10,000 into $783 in a month. At least there was still enough to pay rent.

But you know what? Monday of the following week the Nasdaq soared 217.87 points, or 6.6 percent. That was its largest one-day point gain ever at that time. On Tuesday, the Nasdaq broke Monday's record by rocketing 254.41 points, or 7.2 percent. That was the second-largest one-day percentage gain in history at that time. Perhaps there were more cherries left in the bowl than Alan thought.

If you were a dollar-cost-averager like Merck-investing Larry, that crash week was a great time to send in a few extra bucks. If you were a buy-on-the-dipper, you were hard pressed to find a more suitable dip. The fact that you had plenty of other dips in 2000 and early 2001 leads us nicely into the next section.

Either You Have Lost or You Will Lose

There's one theme you can't miss if you read a bit about the stock market: It ain't an easy way to get rich. In fact, it's downright tough and often feels impossible. That's when bonds get popular and bank certificates of deposit start getting their share of ink in business papers. Unfortunately, stocks go down. You don't know when it's going to happen, and neither do I, and neither does Alan Abelson, although he'll be the first to let you know when they have.

All that being the case, it's a good idea to be careful when you invest. What you thought was a surefire investment might not be. What you thought was the beginning of a new era might not be. What you thought was a great time to finally use that margin feature of your brokerage account might not be. Surefire investments burn up, new eras get old, and margin features result in margin calls.

Wade in, don't dive. That's the lesson learned in the collective experience of most independent investors I know. Dollar-cost averaging is a good way to wade in. You can still focus your portfolio on the top investments that your research turns up, but that doesn't mean you have to pile all of your cash in at once.

Joan Schwarz of Lincoln, Nebraska, was caught by that skydiving market of April 2000. "I'd been watching CMGI for more than a year, never quite having the courage to invest. I was leary of Internet stocks because they were so expensive, but they just kept going up. I saved my extra cash, waiting for the right time to buy. Over the last two weeks of March, CMGI dropped more than 30 percent and was trading at $100 per share. That was my signal so I put all of my cash in, already counting the booty from the recovery. Getting back to its mid-March price of $145 a share would give me a quick 45 percent on my investment. CMGI is the top Internet incubator, so this was a no-lose situation." But, like so many investors who dive into no-lose situations, Joan lost big time. "CMGI went from $100 to $50 in the next two weeks. It made me sick. I wanted to invest more money at the bargain price levels, but I didn't have any more. I invested everything in the first purchase because I thought that was a bargain price."

Notice she wanted to dive into the $50 bargain in April? The $50 bargain became a $30 bargain in September. Time to dive? The $30 bargain became a $15 bargain in November. Surely it's time to dive now. Yet the $15 bargain became a $4 bargain in January 2001. This absolutely has to be the dive bell, right? Wrong. The $4 bargain went on sale for $1.75 on April 6, 2001. Never, never dive in. It can lead to 98 percent losses. Diving is risky.

Broadly speaking, Joan's decision to buy what she considered a top company at a 30-percent discount was a good move. The timing in that case was unfortunate to say the least, but she was lucky that she didn't need the money back right away and could wait while the market and CMGI recovered. Who knows how long that wait will be. At the time of this writing—fourteen months after her purchase—she's still down 97 percent.

The advantages of wading in slowly are too good to pass up. Say she had been investing $10,000. She chose to put it all in at $100 and ended up with 100 shares. If instead she'd invested $2000 at $100, then again at $50, $25, $15, and $5, she'd have ended up with 673 shares. In a recovery back to her initial target of $145, the 100 shares she bought would be worth $14,500 for a gain of 45 percent. Not bad, but the 673 shares that she could have bought gradually would have been worth $97,585 for a gain of 876 percent.

It happens the same way on sells, by the way. Evan Stephens of Denver experienced that problem with Dell. "I owned it for six months, bought at $42. It hovered between $39 and $44 the whole time. I finally sold at $44 and over the next few weeks it went all the way to $55. I should publish a newsletter of my investment moves so people can do the opposite. If I'm buying, you should sell. If I'm selling, you should buy."

Actually, that publication already exists. It's called *Barron's*. It doesn't get everything wrong but enough to make you wonder what Alan Abelson is so smug about. The September 15, 1997, issue wrote of Microsoft's impending collapse from the threat of Java, Sun's programming language. In the two and a half years following the *Barron's* article, Microsoft stock rose some 300 percent, and the company made superb progress in its transition from a PC-centric firm to an Internet-centric one.

But I shouldn't single out *Barron's* or pick on Alan Abelson. Remember, none of us gets it right consistently. I lost big money in my personal portfolio during that black, swirling 2000–2001 bear market. I didn't see it coming. Joan didn't see it coming. Evan didn't see Dell's 25-percent surge coming.

So let's get something straight. There are two kinds of investors: those who *have* lost money and those who *will* lose money. Not overall, we hope, but at some point. Which is why you should learn from the mistakes of others and move gradually. It will minimize your losses when you're wrong, and the fact that you're moving at all will allow you to participate in gains when you're right. Dollar-cost averaging accomplishes this magic automatically, but you should also move gradually when you're investing lump sums. Don't do it all on Tuesday. Keep some cash in case you're wrong because some day you will be.

Pay Small Amounts to Learn

The advantages of moving gradually are pretty well understood at this level of moving into and out of positions. But there's a bigger-picture way to move gradually that involves learning with a small portion of your cash.

Estelle Alford is a 72-year-old grandmother in Pocatello, Idaho. She began investing with her husband Hugh more than forty years ago. Hugh passed away in 1992, and Estelle has managed the family portfolio by herself ever since. She remembers when the two of them were just starting out and hadn't the foggiest idea where to begin. "There were a lot fewer choices back in the '50s and '60s," she remembers. "Hugh liked the radio companies and the automobile makers. I liked steel and oil outfits. Today you can read all kinds of books about investing and listen to the radio for help. We didn't have that back then. There was the *Wall Street Journal*, and that was just for the men working downtown. We were a little scared, so we used just 10 percent of the money we intended to invest. Hugh said that way we could lose it all and still not be doing too badly. We didn't lose it all, but we didn't know what we were doing either."

Estelle's not the only one who advocates starting your investment program with a small amount of money. For *The Neatest Little Guide to Stock Market Investing*, I interviewed Gary Pilgrim, one of my favorite mutual fund managers. His fund, PBHG Growth, averaged 22 percent per year in the ten years ending January 2001, compared to the S&P 500's 17 percent. In our interview, I suggested to Gary that individual investors should begin with 10 percent of their money, take a few knocks, and emerge a wiser investor for the experience. He agreed. "Pay small amounts to learn, not large amounts. . . . Over time, if you develop confidence in your strategy, you can eventually increase the amount of money you actively manage."

The Alfords learned with small amounts of money at a time when there weren't many places to put it. Individual stocks were the whole game, and if you chose the wrong stocks, you were in trouble. Today's investor has more than 13,000 mutual funds to choose from in addition to twice as many individual stocks. Estelle thinks the situation gives beginning investors better odds of success. "Oh, we would be much more comfortable starting today," she told me. "We wouldn't need to go directly from a bank account to individual stocks. We could start with a small amount of money in a mutual fund."

What type of fund? "I think Index mutual funds are the beginner's dream."

Good choice. Being able to buy the stock market for a measly 0.20 percent annual cost is such an opportunity I think everybody should be forced to do it. Reading about the market and theorizing is fine and dandy, but won't get you as far as one month of watching your actual money bounce around. The problem with watching your own money as a beginner is that you can watch it bounce right to zero and end up thinking there's no hope in the giant casino on Wall Street. Discouraged beginners might lose ten years of opportunity just screwing up the courage to try again. An index mutual fund won't go to zero, but it will bounce and jiggle with each new whisper about earnings or statement from the Federal Reserve, neither of which matters in the end. Index funds are a safe way to get the thick skin you need to understand that the market doesn't follow anybody's rules. Once you've got that thick skin and you're used to reading about businesses, you're in a lot better spot to choose individual stocks.

I asked Estelle if she thinks most investors should eventually buy stocks. "Yes, when they finally know what they're doing. For some people that day will never come. I've got a few relatives, bless their hearts, who just can't seem to understand the first thing about investing. So I sent them to Vanguard and got them started in the S&P 500 index fund and told them to keep sending money. End of lesson for them. For others, they eventually felt comfortable with the market and pulled out some money for individual companies like Johnson & Johnson, one I told them about after seeing how many Band-Aids my grandchildren go through."

Why stocks over mutual funds? Because of the tax advantages and because when you finally feel comfortable with the stock market you realize that it's not impossible after all. The house of cards and hall of mirrors reputation is just an illusion that the brokers keep going for their own profit. Fact is, picking companies that are going to make money in the future and buying part of them isn't very hard. Getting it perfectly right is impossible. Getting it right enough to do well over the long term is within anybody's grasp. Just look at Estelle. While CMGI spent the year 2000 dropping from $163 to $6, her Johnson & Johnson suggestion went from $91 to $105.

Stalking the Proper Excuses

Peter Lynch, the former manager of Fidelity Magellan, has explained why individuals have an advantage over professionals when it comes to picking stocks. In his book *One Up on Wall Street*, he wrote these snippets:

> You have to understand the minds of people in our business. We all read the same newspapers and magazines and listen to the same economists. We're a very homogeneous lot, quite frankly. . . .
>
> Under the current system, a stock isn't truly attractive until a number of large institutions have recognized its suitability and an equal number of Wall Street analysts have put it on the recommended list. With so many people waiting for others to make the first move, it's amazing that anything gets bought. . . .
>
> Whoever imagines that the average Wall Street pro-

fessional is looking for reasons to buy exciting stocks hasn't spent much time on Wall Street. The fund manager most likely is looking for reasons *not* to buy exciting stocks so that he can offer the proper excuses if those exciting stocks happen to go up. . . .

In fact, between the chance of making an unusually large profit on an unknown company and the assurance of losing only a small amount on an established company, the normal mutual fund manager, pension fund manager, or corporate portfolio manager would jump at the latter. Success is one thing, but it's more important not to look bad if you fail. . . .

It's no wonder that portfolio managers and fund managers tend to be squeamish in their stock selections. There's about as much job security in portfolio management as there is in go-go dancing and football coaching. Coaches can at least relax between seasons. Fund managers can never relax because the game is played year-round. The wins and losses are reviewed after every third month, by clients and bosses who demand immediate results.

There now, isn't that encouraging? Not if your intention is to be the best investor on your block in the course of your lifetime. However, as Estelle has made clear, mutual funds are a good way to get your investment program off the ground. In the beginning, you're not looking to make history. You're looking to get your feet wet, and funds are a relatively safe way to do so.

Besides, there are actively managed funds that do beat the market. Admittedly, most funds do not for the reasons Peter Lynch outlined, but a percentage of them do, and they're not hard to find. Heck, they're listed in the popular magazines twice a year. Who's on top for the past six months? The magazines will tell you, along with a picture of the smiling fund manager and a few words about his or her extracurricular activities. ("In his spare time, John takes his aggressive stock buying habits to the slopes of Aspen, where he hits the pipe on his custom snowboard." Insert picture of brisk-faced John standing beside snowboard. Six months later, John's fund hasn't returned a penny more and nobody ever hears about him again. This happens all the time.)

As usual, you shouldn't care about the six-month winner. We

all know by now that *somebody* has to win in the short term, but it rarely has much to do with investment acumen. However, you will also conveniently find in roundup features a list of funds that have won over three years, five years, ten years, and occasionally even longer. Those lists are downright handy when you're setting up a long-term investment program and need a couple funds to get started.

The Simplest Investment Plan Ever

Here's the simplest approach to the stock market for everybody who would rather be doing something else:

1. Open an account at Vanguard.
2. Invest every month in the S&P 500 index fund.
3. Have another beer.

I admit it's not challenging and won't give you much to do. You won't have any stories to tell aside from, "Yep, I received my statement again last month." But you'll never underperform the market, you'll pay a tiny 0.20 percent annual expense, and your tax bill will stay small. One day your account will be worth a lot of money and you'll finally see the sheer genius of what you accidentally accomplished.

Follow the three steps. (Feel free to substitute your beverage of choice.)

Do-It-Yourself Investor Tools

An online broker will save you tons of money. Knowing the difference between market orders and limit orders will make your investing career as stress-free as possible. Move gradually into and out of your investments, and keep investing through the ups and downs. The simplest approach is to invest every month in an S&P 500 index fund. If you accomplish all this, you'll have a super portfolio and I'll be jealous.

Chapter Recap

Here's a rundown of what you learned in this chapter.

- **Full-Service Brokers Are Bad:** Avoid full-service brokers because the full service they provide is laughable. They recommend what they're told to recommend, not what they discovered after exhaustive market research. Why pay extra for mediocrity?

- **Discount Brokers Are Good:** Get thee to an online discount broker. A May 2000 study by *Technology Investor* found that online trading shaves up to 99 percent off the full-service price. That's the difference between paying $800 to buy a stock and paying only $8.

- **Understand the Pros and Cons of Market and Limit Orders:** A market order buys or sells now at the current price; a limit order buys or sells at a price you specify and never executes if that price is never reached. You have read the philosophies of a market order investor and a limit order investor. One watches thoroughly researched stocks for the right time to buy, then buys at that time with a market order. The other determines after research the price he is willing to pay, sets that price in a limit order, then stops watching. Which approach is most appealing to you?

- **Don't Spread Your Money Too Thin:** Owning a little of everything will lead to crummy performance and won't protect you in a market downturn. Diversifying protects you against business risk, which is the chance that a company you own will crash and burn. But studies have shown that owning as few as twelve stocks from different industries protects as well against business risk as owning 120 stocks. Choose the best, then concentrate your money on those. That approach has made billions for Warren Buffett.

- **Keep Investing:** When life stinks, invest more money. When life is grand, invest more money. Always invest more money regardless of what the stock market is doing because doing so will force you to buy more shares when prices are low and fewer shares when prices are high.

That's called dollar-cost averaging, and it's the easiest way for any schmo to create a fortune in the stock market. The brainpower required to accomplish this miracle is roughly equivalent to what's needed at a vending machine. Put money in, get something out.

- **Move Gradually:** The day will come when you are wrong about a stock's rising performance, and you'll be glad you didn't shoot your whole wad of money on the first buy. If instead you spent only half, you'd have the other half to buy additional shares at the lower price. It works the same way on sells. If you think you'll never be wrong in your judgment of an investment, then you, my friend, have a very painful lesson on the way. I hear the market's sinister chuckle somewhere behind you as I write. It's eyeing your soft flesh and flexing its jaws. There are two kinds of investors: those who *have* lost money and those who *will* lose money. Not overall, we hope, but at some point. When your day comes, lose as little as possible.

- **Learn Gradually:** When you're just starting out, manage only a portion of your money and that in mutual funds. Don't feel the need to start your investment career by day-trading biotech stocks.

- **Keep It Simple:** The simplest investment plan is to send money every month to the Vanguard S&P 500 index fund. You'll match the market's performance, pay only 0.20 percent each year in fees, and your tax bill will be low. Even a jellyfish can make money this way.

Resources from This Chapter

There are plenty of brokers to get you started on the path to good portfolio management. Here are some good ones.

- **Ameritrade** is my online stock broker, and I'm happy. The trades execute quickly, the real-time quotes are available from every page on the site, and the order screens are simple to follow. Commissions are $8 for market orders and $13 for limit orders. **www.ameritrade.com**

- **E*Trade** is a financial bazaar with everything from banking and bill management to shopping and taxes—Oh yeah, and they can trade stocks and mutual funds too. Commissions are $15 for stocks on the New York Stock Exchange, $20 for Nasdaq stocks and limit orders. There's a graduated pricing menu that decreases your commissions if you trade a lot, but we all know where that gets you. **www.etrade.com**

- **Fidelity** is a top choice if you're looking for a place to assemble a mutual fund portfolio. The company's Funds-Network program gathers leading names into one place, without loads or transaction fees. For stocks, I'd look elsewhere. Commissions are $25 for market orders and $30 for limit orders. (800) 343-3548; **www.fidelity.com**

- **National Discount Brokers** combines the total financial management of E*Trade with the streamlined trading of Ameritrade. Its slick NDB University makes it especially popular among newcomers. A feature I like is that your executed trades are instantly reflected in your portfolio—no waiting for end-of-day accounting. Commissions are $15 for market orders and $20 for limit orders. **www.ndb.com**

- **Schwab** is the leader of them all when judged by customer count. Its OneSource mutual fund supermarket is even better than Fidelity's because it gathers higher quality names. Like Fidelity, however, Schwab is too expensive for stock trading. Commissions are $30. (800) 435-4000; **www.schwab.com**

- **Vanguard** prides itself at keeping expenses low. It pioneered index funds for the masses, thereby giving me the ability to offer you "The Simplest Investment Plan Ever" on page 116. You can't find a better place than Vanguard for low-cost, long-term mutual fund investing. Getting started in the S&P 500 index fund (symbol VFINX) is free, and the annual cost is only 0.20 percent. The national average cost is 1.25 percent. (800) 871-3879; **www.vanguard.com**

6 / Finding $500 per Month

You need money to get your investments started and money to keep them going. A brokerage account with no money is a car with no gas, a plane with no wings, a bicycle with no tires. With enough gas, wings, and tires you'll be rich in no time.

I know what you're thinking: "This seems an odd place to put the chapter on finding money to invest. Shouldn't this have been Chapter 1?" Logically, yes, it should have, and you'll notice that it *is* the first item on the list of "Ten Steps to Do-It-Yourself Investing" at the front of the book. But in my experience people get much more excited about the mechanics of the market, the drama of fortunes made and lost, and the wee potential of triple-digit returns. They want that stuff up front to get their blood pumping. Only later, in somber moments, does it occur to them that they have to take care of some preliminary steps first, like opening a brokerage account and finding an extra $500 per month. So that's why you and I are just now getting around to this step, even though it'll actually be the first thing you do. Blame it on all those average readers.

There are publications telling you that all it takes is $25 a month to reach your financial goals. Maybe, if you have small goals or lots of time and don't mind using all of it waiting. I consider investing $500 per month to be a solid target. That puts $6000 per year toward your dreams, which, invested wisely, can turn into a princely sum quickly. A heck of a lot quicker than

$300 per year anyway. So let's find you an extra $500 every month to invest.

Trim the Fat and Send It In

The easiest way to make extra money is to avoid spending what you already have. You save small money by cutting small expenses and big money by cutting big expenses. Repetitive big expenses are the best targets of all. Your biggest expenses are probably taxes, housing, transportation, and food. You save most on taxes by starting your own business, something I'll discuss later. As for the others, let's tackle them right here.

Renting from Ron, Buying from Dick

"When I saw how much I was spending on rent, I looked all over town for a cheaper place," says Erica Orovitz of San Jose, California. She found that place, and coincidentally, it ended up being owned by Ron, the investor who warned you in Chapter 2 about the difficulties of real estate ownership. "It killed me to see nearly 40 percent of my take-home pay going toward housing," Erica continues. "I ignored the articles in the paper lamenting the absence of affordable housing in the Bay Area. Through friends, I heard about a charming little place not far from Valley Fair Mall—one of San Jose's most popular shopping areas—that cost less than half of what I was paying for a one-bedroom apartment. I was doubtful but checked it out. It has a tiny front yard, private driveway, laundry room, living room, the works. And it's less than half the cost of an apartment! There was no decision to be made. I moved in."

Now she pays a monthly rent that's extremely cheap for the Bay Area and even below the national average. Compared to what the local cost of living says she should pay for her current home, Erica saves $600 per month. Right there, she's carved out more than enough to start an investment program that will make her financially comfortable.

"People at work can't believe it," she told me. "They say I

got lucky. But it wasn't entirely luck. I set out to find an affordable, nice place to live. I found it. Since moving in there, I've spoken with Ron and my neighbors and discovered a whole list of affordable properties. All you have to do is keep looking." The savings Erica achieved are huge, but even a $100 or $200 savings off the rental payment adds up. In a year, $200 a month turns into $2,400. That's a lot.

I experienced a similar situation in Los Angeles when I bought my home. The rents in L.A. are high too, and I paid the market rate when I first moved to town. After a few years, I knew the city better and had a feel for where I wanted to live. I set a price target and a quality standard, then hit the newspaper for a house. Ten circled addresses later, I began driving around neighborhoods. The first five I eliminated without stopping the car. The others required a walk around. One place looked promising but failed in the end when I stood in the front yard for ten minutes, listening. Too many dogs barking, too many engines revving, too many planes overhead.

I mentioned to friends that I hadn't found any suitable homes in my price range. "You know," said one, "my neighbor is thinking of selling his place, and it's a heck of a good home. We've seen them repainting and carpeting and planting flowers to get it ready to sell. You should take a look." I made the drive and found a quaint home behind a white fence. Rising from the front flowerbed was a mailbox just waiting for my name on it. The home has a garage, beautiful landscaping, and even a fountain. From the bedroom, I could see the lights of downtown Los Angeles. A window in the home office provided a hillside view through the branches of a tangerine tree. Everything was clean. The shades opened smoothly, the garbage disposal worked, the carpet was brand new. And I liked the owner, Dick Sherman, whom you met back in Chapter 2.

Dick's asking price was 25 percent lower than comparable properties, which is a strange term to use because I didn't find many of the supposedly comparable ones near as appealing. I didn't even bargain on the price. Well, not much. I asked Dick for a couple thousand off to help pay for escrow and a few items I wanted to buy. He said sure. The whole deal happened with a handshake. No realtor. No listings. No offers or counters. Dick and I drove to the escrow office to sign papers, then shared coffee and pie at his favorite restaurant. Cutting out the realtor saved more than $10,000.

The point is not that you should call Dick for affordable property in Los Angeles, but that good deals in housing are available. Erica found a bargain in the most expensive real estate market in the country, such a bargain that it's even cheap by the standards in your town. I can write that confidently because her monthly payment is well below the national average. I found a bargain in another expensive market. In both cases, the tenant and buyer relied on nontraditional research to get where they wanted to be. Erica asked friends and networked her way to properties not listed in the newspaper. I did the same. We both saved a lot, and you can too.

"But," you say, "I'm happy right where I live. I don't want to pull up stakes and move across town just to save a few hundred dollars a month." Fair enough. Let's discuss that car in your driveway.

The $45,894 Honda

If you bought your car new with financing for more than $20,000 then you just discovered a major savings opportunity. If your spouse is driving a second car with an equally high price tag, you might be staring at a driveway worth $500 per month when you replace those vehicles with better bargains.

"I bought a 1999 Honda Accord for $21,950," reports Marjorie Rothweis of Watertown, New York. "Adding 7-percent tax brought the total to $23,487. I put $4,697 down and financed the rest at 8 percent for 36 months. My payments are $589." The money going toward that Honda is an investment program waiting to happen, and it's not even a fancy car. It's nice but not the kind of car you park on the far side of the lot so that nobody opens a door into the side of it.

"I thought of financing for a five-year term to bring down the payments, but five years seemed like so long." It is, especially when you're paying $381 per month the whole time, which is what it would have cost. When she finally owned the car at the end of five years, it wouldn't have been new anymore. So what would she have done then? Probably buy another one.

"Why did you buy a new car in the first place?" I asked.

"Because I needed reliable transportation. Hondas are safe, and they had a sale going that day. I liked the way it felt. I could picture it in my driveway, and I wanted it right then." And hopefully for the next three years and more. How much difference do you think there is between the 1999 model and the 1998? How about the 1997? Not much. Marjorie herself said that Hondas are reliable. She should have noticed that a two-year-old Honda runs well, is just as safe as the brand-new one and costs considerably less.

Better yet, she could have gone back five years. That seems ancient to some people, but is outright sparkling to others. Merton Howell of Vermillion, South Dakota, drives a ten-year-old Celica that he bought two years ago out of the newspaper. "I like my Celica," he told me. "It's got a sunroof, and the radio sounds good. It's a great car. I paid $3,500 for it, and all I've had to do is change belts and oil— Oh, and the alternator gave out a while back. That cost me $200."

Let's compare Merton's situation to Marjorie's. He paid $3,500 one time to own the car outright. She paid a $4,697 down payment and needs to pay another $589 every month for the next three years. He needs to change the oil regularly; she needs to change the oil regularly. Their cars get roughly the same fuel economy. He had to pay $200 for a new alternator. Any alternator trouble she has in the next three years is covered by warranty. Neither mentioned this next part, but I will. His insurance is about $550 per year; hers is about $1,300. His car gets him to and from work every day; her car gets her to and from work every day.

Let's assume clever Merton uses the $500 per month he's saving to invest in an S&P 500 index fund for the next three years, the term of Marjorie's loan. After three years, Marjorie owns a 1999 Honda Accord that is worth 40 percent less than what she paid for it. By the way, because she financed the car, it ended up costing a total of $25,894, *not* the pre-tax sticker price of $21,950. That's an important $3,944 difference. The difference between the Honda's sticker price and the actual price Marjorie paid over three years is more than enough to purchase Merton's Celica!

So she's got her depreciated Honda after three years. Meanwhile, Merton's $6,000 per year invested at the market's historic

11-percent annual return is worth more than $20,000. Plus, he has his Celica, which is worth a full 85 percent of what he paid for it. Put this way, Marjorie's Honda cost her the $25,894 price plus the $20,000 missed investment opportunity. That's a $45,894 Honda she's driving. I hope she likes it.

The lesson here is clear. You save a ton of money driving a used car that's paid for. It'll get you where you need to go and should be able to do so in fine style. To quote *The Neatest Little Guide to Personal Finance*:

> Every new car will one day be a used car. The question is, will it become a used car on your tab or somebody else's?

"That's interesting," you mutter as you sit reading this in the passenger seat of your new BMW while your spouse drives, "but we like our leather seating surfaces and our individual climate controls. What's more, we don't mind paying $848 per month to have them. Next idea?"

Food on the Floor

Okay, how about the food in your kitchen? If you are loyal to national brands and buy only what you need when you need it, you're probably overspending at the grocery store each month by at least $100.

"I've tried clipping coupons from the Sunday paper, but it's a hassle," complains May Farnum of Columbia, South Carolina. She takes care of her three children ages 10, 8, and 4, while her husband Lou runs a window glass company. "Lou watched my clipping routine, and he noticed that what I bought depended on the coupons I found that week. Forty cents off seems like a bargain, but it isn't if you're buying something you wouldn't otherwise buy. After that revelation, I tried making my weekly shopping list before scanning the paper for coupons. That worked better, but the time I put into it was hardly worth the eight or ten coupons I'd find that matched items on my list." Finding eight or ten is doing better than most people. I found some interesting shopping information from an accounting firm that advises grocery stores. Evidently, the average Sunday paper contains a hundred or more coupons, but most readers looking for deals clip only three to six coupons for products they really want and use. There must be a better way.

Lou found it. His job involves figuring out the most efficient type of window glass to keep a building heated or cooled for minimal expense. He likes to research small cost savings like that and decided to do it on the family grocery tab. He kept a journal of their receipts for a few months as May experimented with different types of buying. He found that she spent the same amount on groceries whether she clipped coupons for food they wouldn't have otherwise bought or clipped just the handful of coupons that matched their shopping list. Either way they spent $500 per month.

Then May switched to a system where she didn't use coupons at all, but just found the cheapest brand of every item on her list. No brand loyalty was the only rule. That took her into store brands and generic labels, the stuff either high or low on the shelves. After a couple trips she found which of the cheaper brands were of high enough quality to become regulars in her kitchen. If ever a different brand of sufficient quality would go on sale at a cheaper price, she'd buy that one instead. Remember, no brand loyalty. If the item on sale was something her family continually used, like canned corn, she would buy in bulk. This system brought their monthly grocery bill down to $375 per month, and May doesn't mess with coupons anymore.

The national brands with their appealing label designs are often selling the same products as the store brands. The colors are the same, the textures are the same, the taste is the same. The only difference is the cost and shelf location.

> Of course, everybody has their preferences. Some people swear by certain national brands and switching to what they consider an inferior store brand just to save 20 cents would be stupid. Life should be enjoyed. What I'm advocating here is that you experiment a little to find the cheaper products that are enjoyable to you and your family. I found a store brand vanilla yogurt that I like better than any national brand yogurt. I love it. It tastes so good it's like ice cream, yet it costs half of what the national brands cost and is low fat too.

That's the way it is with products like shaving cream and toothpaste and deodorant and breakfast cereal. Have you ever tried some of those bags of cereal on the floor shelf of the grocery aisle? The names are silly, but they taste good. Stick with May's system. Reach a little in the grocery store instead of keeping your arms at eye level and you too may enjoy an instant 25-percent savings every month. For May, that turned into $1,200 a year and she saves time that she used to spend clipping coupons.

"Look," you sigh, "I'm not stooping to the floor shelf for a bag of cereal. I like my expensive house, I love my brand-new car, and I like eating name brand cereal from boxes shelved at eye level. Do you have any other ways to save a buck?" Indeed I do.

Suite Long-Distance Rates

You know that innocent-looking phone on your wall? It's probably costing you $25 to $50 more per month than it should. Let me guess: You signed up for one of those flat 9 cents per minute long-distance plans with a $5 monthly fee, and you're feeling good.

Check out OneSuite.com, a prepaid long-distance provider. You use your credit card at the website to add money to your account. When you want to place a call, you dial a toll-free access number, enter your PIN, and dial the number you're calling. There's a nifty feature called ZipDial that lets you specify up to three phone lines from which you don't even need to dial the PIN. If you've signed up for ZipDial and are calling from one of the specified lines, you simply dial the toll-free access number and the number you're calling.

OneSuite.com

There's no monthly fee. Any calls in the forty-eight states are 2.9 cents per minute, 24 hours a day. Alaska and Hawaii are 10 cents. Italy is 11.5 cents, Japan is 6.5 cents, and the United Kingdom is 5 cents. It's tough to beat those prices. Anywhere you go in the country, you can pick up a phone and use your OneSuite account to place a call over the toll-free line at these rates. It's better than a standard long-distance service and much better than a calling card.

You might think you're getting a deal with a promotional 9-cent flat rate. Let's say that in one month you talk for 300 minutes on calls within the forty-eight states. That'll cost you $27.00 on the 9-cent plan, but only $8.70 on the OneSuite plan. Plus, you'll probably have to pay a $3 or $5 monthly fee with the 9-cent plan.

And don't complain about the extra step of dialing the toll-free access number. If you have speed dial buttons on your phone, the process will add a mere two seconds to the front of your phone call. That's a pretty minimal effort to save 68 percent on your long-distance.

The 40-Year Sofa Purchase Plan

Just because you're paying your long-distance with a credit card doesn't mean you should run a tab on that card. Pay off your cards every month. Why, surely by now you've realized that you can't get ahead investing for an 11 percent return while paying debt interest at 18 percent. (Or higher—I've seen some cards with rates of 22 percent.)

"I bought new furniture on our Visa card three years ago," recalls Martha Jeffries of Alamogordo, New Mexico. "The cost was $3,500 and I'm still paying. I had to finally get rid of the card to keep from spending more, but I still carry that debt. I should have it paid off within a year or so." If she paid 18 percent a year on that $3,500 and sent just the minimum payment each month, it would take her forty years to pay off the furniture and would cost an extra $9,431 in interest on top of the $3,500 owed.

Look, if you're trying to become an investor, you need to think like one, and an investor doesn't waste ten grand over forty years. The debt is bad enough but the opportunity cost is almost more of a shame. If you took five years to pay off a $4,000 credit card balance in the late 1990s, you missed out on one of the best runs in the market. That money could have been worth $20,000 by 2000.

Even outside those golden years, however, the point holds true. If you take five years to pay off $4000 at 22 percent interest, you will pay $110 per month for sixty months. That's a total of

$6,600. You lose not only the $6,600 of interest expense, you also miss out on the $8,747 you would have had by investing $110 every month for sixty months at an 11 percent annual return. Paying off your credit cards is a risk-free, tax-free, guaranteed way to earn 18 to 22 percent on your money year after year. That's an investment record even Warren Buffett would respect.

Low Odds, Low Premiums

The last thing you want to think about is a fire sweeping through your home, turning to ash everything you hold dear. But it happens, and it might happen to you. That's why it's smart to insure your home, your car, and sometimes your income—which is the only thing life insurance preserves— You didn't think it preserved your life, did you? You know about insurance, of course, and you're probably so keenly aware of life's dangers that you've insured yourself from attic to tire iron with the shiniest policies ever put to paper. That could be a big mistake. You might be overspending.

Take the highest possible deductible on your insurance policies and you'll lower your payments dramatically. To understand the wisdom of this approach, consider how the insurance industry works. In order for the insurance industry to survive, it has to pay out far less than it takes in. Insurance is only offered when the odds of an accident are low. It can't work any other way, right? If the odds of paying out are high, the insurance company won't make money. The more you think about it, the more you realize that the odds are against your ever needing to use your insurance policies, and you should therefore pay as little for them as possible.

When you take the highest deductible—that is, the amount you need to pay in the event of a claim before the insurance company starts paying—your scheduled insurance payments decrease.

I know a woman who saved $1,000 per year just by converting from comprehensive auto insurance to liability with the highest deductible. Her driving record is good and her car is a few years old now, so she's confident that she'll have the money to repair it if she ever gets into an accident. That's a big if, as you know after thinking about how the insurance industry works.

It works the same way with homeowner's insurance. Take the

highest deductible and stop playing with matches in the living room.

I have a list of affordable insurance companies for you. Check prices for auto policies with Amica (800) 992-6422, Colonial Penn (800) 847-1729, and Geico (800) 841-3000. If you're an active-duty or retired military officer, or a dependent of one, try USAA (800) 531-8080. If you live in California, try 21st Century (800) 211-7233. Finally, InsWeb offers free quotes from all different companies at its website, **www.insweb.com**. You fill out a profile one time, then click to see the best rates for you in auto, home, life, and health insurance. Choose the cheapest policy and you're done.

> **21st Century**
> **Amica**
> **Colonial Penn**
> **Geico**
> **InsWeb**
> **USAA**

Life insurance is a financial minefield because it involves money left to your family after you die.

Your feelings about the subject of death are powerful, and every life insurance sales force loves that. Those emotions are tied to the people you leave behind. But if there's nobody left behind, you don't need any insurance, as explained in this excerpt from *The Neatest Little Guide to Personal Finance*:

> Now, you can see that life insurance has nothing to do with your life except that it cashes in when you cash out. It exists to save your dependents, which leads to the most important lesson about life insurance: If you don't have any dependents, you don't need life insurance. If you are single and the only person who depends on you is you, then you've read all you need to read about life insurance. Congratulations. You just saved a bundle.

If you do have dependents, you should go with term life insurance, not whole. Term insurance is best because it protects you for a certain period of time, after which you can renew for another term. You buy only what you need, and there's no cash value to worry about. It's just pure coverage. It's affordable, too. A 30-year-old nonsmoker would pay about $250 per year for a benefit of $100,000. The price goes up every time the policy is renewed for another term because the chances of death increase. The price becomes most expensive very late in life, and it's that fact that is the best angle insurance reps will use to convince you to go with whole life.

They tell you that you might not be able to afford the steep payments when you get old. What they leave out is that you probably won't need any life insurance when you get old because your children will (I hope) support themselves by then, and you and your spouse will (I hope) have saved enough money for either one of you to survive alone. You know another small detail the sales reps leave out when they're convincing you to go with whole life insurance instead of term? That whole pays them eight times the commission term pays.

Go with term, and shop for the most affordable policy from SelectQuote (800) 343-1985 and Termquote (800) 444-8376. Also, don't forget to check InsWeb at **www.insweb.com**.

> **SelectQuote**
> **TermQuote**

I could go on about other moneysaving ideas, but you probably get the picture. If you find cheaper housing, drive a pre-owned car, cut your food bills, pay 2.9 cents per minute for your long-distance, eliminate your credit card balances, and take the maximum deductible on your insurance policies, you should be able to free up the $500 per month needed for a solid investment program. If not, don't despair—there are other ways to get the money. Start by reading *The Neatest Little Guide to Bank Robbery, Drug Dealing, and Embezzlement.*

Let the Good Times Pay

You can always work for the money, an old-fashioned idea, I know. You probably already have a job or some form of income. If after cutting obvious expenses you still can't find the full $500 every month, consider getting an additional job. I'm not talking about filling every second of your free time with drudgery so burdensome that you lie awake at night pondering the meaning of life. I'm talking about turning recreation into profits.

Paddling for Profit

Patrick McMordie of San Jose, California, works full time as an engineer for JSR Microelectronics. On weekends, he drives 130 miles to the three forks of the American river near Sacramento where he works as a whitewater rafting guide. "I went rafting for the first time nine years ago with a group from my company. I enjoyed it so much that I came three other times that summer. I got to know a few of the guides during lunches and on quiet parts of the river. They said the company runs a guide school every spring and that they offer part time work. The following April, I showed up at guide school." What used to cost Pat $125 a day to enjoy now pays him about $70 a day, including tips. "Plus I get free meals," he says. "I have to prepare them myself on the side of a river, but they're free."

Look at everything Pat's getting from this arrangement. He enjoys rafting, so the weekend is an escape from his regular job. It's an outdoor, physical activity that keeps him healthy. He's made new friends who work for the rafting company and others he met as guests. In addition to all these nonfinancial rewards, Pat takes home an extra $560 per month for five months out of the year. "It doesn't even feel like work," he told me. "I never count on the money. I just drive to the river, have a great time on the water with people I like, and return to San Jose ready to take on another workweek. When the paycheck shows up in the mail, it's just an added bonus."

Five-Star Cash

So additional job tip number one is, Head to the countryside. Tip number two? Head to the city.

I visited one of downtown L.A.'s five-star hotels. I chatted with the doorman helping visitors from their cars to the building. He never carries bags. Another team handles that. His job is to simply greet people, help them from the car, and be friendly. He told me he took the job as a way to get out of the house on weekends and meet exciting people doing interesting things.

"Like what?" I asked him.

"Like coming to the United States for the first time to practice English, or to look for merchandise to export, or to compete in an international dance competition. Everybody in the world passes through L.A. The ones who come to this hotel regularly have become friends. They bring me gifts from other countries and invite me to dinner now and then. All I have to do is welcome them and help them with any problems they might have. I signal taxis, close passenger doors, find attractions on maps, give directions, stuff like that. It's fun and it pays well."

"Oh?" I rudely inquired. "How well?"

He pulled wads of cash from both front pockets. "It's eight p.m. and I'll be here until midnight. I'm halfway through my shift. This is around $80, and that's light. We haven't had much traffic yet." On a typical night, it turns out, he collects $200 in tips. A single here, five bucks there, and by the time he's done making new friends, he goes home with an extra $200. He works every Friday and every other Saturday. That's $1200 a month before his hourly paycheck. This is work anybody can do.

Getting Paid to Sleep

Maybe you don't live near a rafting river or a five-star hotel in one of the world's most trafficked cities. Have no fear, there's part-time work in your neck of the woods too.

Elizabeth Lauder of Allenspark, Colorado, wanted money to invest. She had cut all the unnecessary expenses to the point where she used extra shelving in the basement of her home to store bulk grocery purchases. As a single mother of seven children, four of whom still live at home, she didn't want to get a full-time job away from the family. "I worked in a doctor's office when I was in my twenties and enjoyed it," she told me. "I thought that would be a good place to work again, but the hours would take me away from my family during the week. My youngest son hasn't started kindergarten yet, and I refuse to put him in daycare. I searched for a job that would let me work at night, when the older kids are home and can babysit. Even that didn't sit well with me, however, because I wanted to spend time with them too." An impossible situation for some, but not for this determined lady.

"I found a home-care company in Longmont that staffs homes of four to eight disabled people. They offered late-night shifts that allow workers to sleep on the premises, as long as they're easily awakened should the patients need help during the night. I like my coworkers, and it makes me feel good to help the patients in need. I'm away just two nights per week, and it's during the time that my children are asleep anyway. I have a part-time job that results in almost no time away from the family." For much of the time she's at the home-care facility, Elizabeth sleeps. Now this is a good job. She's going to sleep anyway, so why not get paid for it? At a rate of $15 per hour, she's getting paid pretty well.

"I like this job for several reasons. The time it allows me to spend with my family is the most important. Then there's the good feeling I get helping people in need. I've made new friends because I like my coworkers. All this, and I have money to invest for retirement." Actually, more than that. Working two nights per week, Elizabeth takes home $720 every month after taxes. After socking away $500 of it for retirement, she's left with an extra $220 for the home. "That money I save for vacations. Once a year we all pile into the car and go somewhere together for a week."

It seems that no matter where you live or how complicated your situation is, there's a part-time job available for you. Choose something enjoyable, and make money doing it.

Become a Baron, Magnate, or Tycoon

If there's something you've always dreamed of doing for money and nobody offers it, why not create it for yourself? Operating your own business—even part-time out of your home—can provide the extra money you need to invest. It also creates tax advantages and opens better retirement account options. Not to mention that it's a thrill and will make you proud to succeed.

Child Fun and Mommy Money

Just ask Jenny Wanderscheid, a woman I met while researching an article about successful online businesses. The last thing I expected to hear when calling the office of a successful online business was the sound of children. But that was the background noise at ChildFun.com as I spoke with Jenny, the owner and a 29-year-old mother of three children ages 7, 5, and 2. She started the website from her house in Mankato, Minnesota, to help other stay-at-home mothers. The homepage immediately asks the question, "Who says parenting can't be fun?"

Just a few years ago, Jenny's husband, Rick, was working eighty hours a week building telecommunications equipment in a local factory. Jenny wanted to take some pressure off her husband, who was earning all the money to pay down their mounting credit card bills, but she refused to turn her children over to daycare. To earn money from home, she tried several business opportunities out of the classified ads and briefly experimented with making barrettes. Nothing worked.

In 1997, Jenny went online and found a smattering of websites with tips for stay-at-home mothers. She collected those links on a homepage called "Tigger's Place" after her nickname, and hosted the site on a local service with a crummy address ending in /~mrsrickw instead of a traditional dot com address. The site was so amateurish that visitors couldn't even click the links. "You had to highlight them with your mouse, copy them, and paste them into your browser," she remembers. "It's so embarrasing to think that I called it a website." More mothers learned of Jenny's fledgling page and she soon counted between 1,000 and 2,000 visitors a month, every one of them copying and pasting the links to visit Jenny's recommended sites.

Then one day, the first sign of e-commerce showed up. "I saw an ad for eToys showing that they sold Tickle Me Elmo dolls. I thought that would be a good item for my audience, so I called eToys and asked how I could point people to the toy. They sent me a link and I put it on the page, never even realizing that I'd get paid for the sales." That link produced a $500 check in just three months. "That was around Christmas time, so we spent the money on the kids and a heating bill. After that, I told Rick that we should get one of those domain name things. We could make serious money at this, like $200 per month for groceries!"

Ah, the innocence. The money needed to register the domain name, better known as the ubiquitous dot com address, had already been spent on Christmas presents and the heating bill. Not to be deterred, Jenny sold plasma from her own blood twice a week at $20 a visit to raise money for the address. So much for the theory that you need millions of venture capital dollars to succeed online. If it took selling plasma to purchase **www.childfun.com**, I shuddered to think what Jenny went through to pay for marketing and advertising. Donating organs?

"Of course not," she chirped. "I've never paid for traffic. I considered it now and again, but I'm such a cheapskate that I decided against it, and I don't think it's hurt the site one bit." Neither do I. In December 1998 she counted 20,000 visitors. In February 2000 she counted 100,000. In January 2001 she counted 350,000. People visit ChildFun.com for its 1,000-plus pages of articles, craft ideas, a list of product recalls, seasonal songs, and family life cartoons. In Spring 1999 Jenny sent her main e-mail newsletter to 250 subscribers and thought that was a lot. In January 2001 it went to more than 20,000 people.

Jenny's income fluctuates, but she made $5,000 in December 2000. The money comes from ad revenue, which she earns by displaying banners on every page, and affiliate programs like that initial eToys link. She finds products that appeal to her audience, then joins the affiliate programs to earn commissions. Two thirds of the site's revenue comes from ads and one third from commerce. "The site has pushed us into a new tax bracket," she says. "We've paid off all our credit cards and old bills. Only the mortgage, car payments, and a home improvement loan remain. We bought some toys to celebrate, fun stuff like a fishing boat, police scanner, CD burner, and a camera. The income from the site grows every month, but my workload never increases."

Just how much work is that? Depends on the month. "When I was first starting," she says, "I worked my butt off. I was writing articles, getting articles from other mothers, taking care of the kids, learning how to design, and everything else. Today, it's more relaxed. I design everything in Claris Homepage and spend about sixty hours per week on the site. But in January, I worked maybe a total of two hours the whole month. When people e-mailed to ask if they'd been taken off the list by mistake, I was honest and told them I was just lazy and hadn't sent anything."

World headquarters is a desk against one wall of her living room. Neighbors have no idea that a booming Internet business hums across the phone lines from the ordinary starter home containing three bedrooms, a garage with two cars, and a Hewlett-Packard computer storing the site files.

There's real money to be made online, as Jenny's story shows. It's not easy, nothing worthwhile ever is, but it's possible. You won't find a business more flexible with your schedule than one you run online. In fact, I know a fun paperback that will have your website up and running within a couple weeks. It's called *The Neatest Little Guide to Making Money Online*, and the book's realistic goal is to make you an extra $500 per month with affiliate product sales and advertising on a site you design yourself from home. That's precisely the amount I'd like to see you invest every month. Coincidence? You decide.

Dollops of Paint and the Color of Cash

Not everybody wants to run a virtual business. Some prefer the real thing. Spike Dolomite of Tarzana, California, began a business from home that's as hands-on as business gets. She runs an art school from a converted shed in her backyard. "I've always been an artist," she told me. "It's almost impossible to make a living at it, but I was determined. I started by painting signs for businesses. I branched from that into drawing cartoons for ads and logos. It was a tiny side business, though. I never made enough to pay the bills."

Spike's husband, David, is a senior computer network analyst at Universal Studios. He earns enough to keep the family afloat, but with L.A.'s high cost of living, there was little left at the end of the month to invest. Spike wanted to do something to change that, and she wanted it to involve art.

She spent a year as an assistant preschool teacher at a place called the Farm School. She focused on art, and made several good contacts that she would use later when starting her own art classes for children. "I realized that all I wanted to do was teach art to my own son and other children. I left the Farm School and invited other parents to bring their kids to my kitchen for an hour and a half twice per week. That first summer, I had six students and plenty of others on a waiting list. I kept the program going and presented it to the Farm School. Through the school's enrichment program, I received referrals and was able to retain the entire tuition, which was $50 per student."

As the money accumulated, Spike eyed the unused storage shed in the backyard. David was enthusiastic about developing the business to its full potential, so the couple decided to turn the shed into an art school. "Using the money I'd made so far," Spike recalls, "we hired a guy to put in some drywall, a floor, lights, and an air conditioner. I can fit six children at a time. I charge $50 per child and have four classes per week. The classes last for one month, so I gross $1,200 per month before taxes."

Both Jenny Wanderscheid and Spike Dolomite are doing well by doing good, and they're doing it on their own terms. Jenny helps mothers care for their children in fun ways, while Spike teaches children the beauty of art. Each mother is making money at it, far more than the measly $500 per month I would like to see everybody invest.

A Better Break Than Getting Elected to Congress

The money alone is good, but operating your own business is financially helpful at tax time as well because you can deduct business expenses from your income. From *The Neatest Little Guide to Personal Finance*:

> Tax laws were written for people in business. As an employee, you can't deduct much of anything from your income. As a businessperson, you can deduct almost everything. Buying a new computer? If you use it for business, you can deduct the cost from your income. Driving across town for supplies? As long as they're used in your business, you can deduct the mileage from your income.

Nearly any expense you incur in the process of conducting business is deductible.

The money you earn from your business along with the tax breaks created by your business do some real magic on your personal bottom line. Plus, there's the added bonus of being able to sock more away in a tax-deferred retirement account. Regular individual retirement accounts allow you to save only $2,000 per year for retirement, but a simplified employee pension lets you contribute up to 13.04 percent to a maximum of $22,500 each year. You deduct that contribution from your income, which immediately cuts your tax bill. It will feel good putting away a sizable amount for retirement instead of just $2000.

There you have it. The extra $500 per month you need for investing can come from your own business. No other source of income feels better, has as much earnings potential, or brings greater tax benefits. Well, actually, getting elected to Congress does—but you wouldn't stoop that low would you?

Do-It-Yourself Investor Tools

Investments need a steady supply of cash in the account. A brokerage account with no money is a car with no gas, a plane with no wings, a bicycle with no tires. With enough gas, wings, and tires you'll be rich in no time. Your goal is to save or make an extra $500 per month to put toward your investments. With a little creativity, you can do it.

Chapter Recap

Here's a rundown of what you learned in this chapter.

- **Change Your Housing Situation:** You might be able to save the whole $500 per month just by changing your housing situation. Do some creative research. Find a bargain rental by talking to friends, people on street corners, the weird guy in the dark cubicle. Find a home for sale by owner. Because your housing bill repeats every month and is one of your biggest expenses, any savings will add up in a hurry. So hurry.

- **Drive a Used Car:** It can mean the difference between being permanently in debt or permanently ahead. Cars have been made so well for the past ten years that it's easy to get reliable, fun transportation for 30 percent of what you'll pay at the new car lot. Look in the newspaper. Remember, every new car will one day be a used car. The question is, will it become a used car on your tab or somebody else's?

- **Get Ahead in the Grocery Store:** Do not stay loyal to any brand in the grocery store unless you can't live without it. Buy what's on sale, and reach higher or lower than eye level to get better prices. This system is superior to coupon clipping and takes no extra time. A family in South Carolina saved 25 percent this way, which added up to $1,200 per year. Invested at the market's historical average of 11 percent, fellow eater, that becomes $77,000 in twenty years. Experiment with cheaper brands. You'll be well compensated.

- **Long-Distance Savings:** Make your long-distance phone calls with OneSuite.com. It can be used from any phone and costs only 2.9 cents per minute in the forty-eight states, with no monthly fee.

- **Zero Balance Credit Cards:** Ever thought of paying off your credit cards? Do it. If you're charged 18 percent a year on a $3,500 balance and send just the minimum payment each month, it will take forty years to pay down and cost an extra $9,431 interest on top of the $3,500 owed. Come on.

- **High Insurance Deductibles:** Take the highest possible deductible on your insurance policies because the chance of ever needing to use your insurance is low. That's why they insure you in the first place. You can save $1,000 per year just by switching from comprehensive auto insurance to liability with the highest deductible. It's another way that driving a used car pays.

- **Term Life Insurance:** If you need life insurance, get term. It's cheap and you buy only what you need. If you don't have any human dependents, you don't need any life insurance. What's your dog going to do with a million dollars?

- **Turning Pleasure to Profit:** You can always take a second job for extra money, but make it something you enjoy. Turn your recreation to income. There are people guiding whitewater rafting trips, meeting exotic travelers at fancy hotels, and taking care of the disabled. They're getting paid to do it, and they're having a good time. Join them!

- **Start Your Own Business:** Starting your own business can be the most fulfilling way of all to make a few bucks. You get to choose exactly what you do, so dreams are a possibility. You make money. You get tax deductions that employees don't, and you have a nice choice of retirement accounts. These benefits are yours even if it's a part-time business.

Resources from This Chapter

Here are some companies that will help you save money.

- **OneSuite.com** is one of the cheapest long distance companies around. Anywhere in the 48 states is just 2.9 cents per minute and the international rates are a bargain too. You go to the website and pay in advance with a credit card. To make calls, you dial a toll-free number and enter a PIN. You can use it from any phone, so say goodbye to expensive calling cards. **www.onesuite.com**

- **Insurance for your car and home** will probably be cheapest from Amica, Colonial Penn, or Geico. If you're an active duty or retired military officer, or a dependent of one, try USAA. If you live in California, try 21st Century. *Contact information:* Amica, (800) 992-6422, **www.amica.com**; Colonial Penn, (800) 847-1729, **www.geautoinsurance.com**; Geico, (800) 841-3000, **www.geico.com**; USAA, (800) 531-8080, **www.usaa.com**; 21st Century, (800) 211-7233, **www.21stcentins.com**

- **Life insurance** is only necessary if you have human dependents, and even then you should only get term life insurance. Get quotes from SelectQuote and Termquote. SelectQuote, (800) 343-1985, www.selectquote.com; Termquote, (800) 444-8376, www.term-quote.com

- **InsWeb** is an online insurance marketplace where you fill out a profile on yourself one time and get quotes for all kinds of insurance, like home, auto, and life. Just to cover all the bases, be sure to run yourself through its system after getting a few quotes elsewhere. What the heck, it's free. www.insweb.com

7 / And You're Off!

That's most of what you need to get ahead, so I'll get out of the way. Before I finish, I want to tell you about one last person, a delightful young woman named Sharlene Choy. She's a mutual fund investor I met at one of my seminars a few years back. In February 2000 she took me to lunch and brought her portfolio. I pored over statements from her Schwab account.

In September 1997, she opened her account with $7,568 split among three mutual funds: Janus Overseas, Oakmark Select, and PBHG Technology & Communications. She then sent $100 per month to each fund. In February 2000, she sent an additional $3,000 and made a few trades. Adding up her initial balance, monthly contributions, and the lump sum gives her an amount invested of $19,268. Her net portfolio value in February 2000 was $48,199. That's a 150 percent gain in 29 months.

Now, Sharlene is no investment whiz. She just wrote down the names of a few funds she heard mentioned in the seminar, started an investment program, and kept sending money. Every month she'd get her statements and write an up or down arrow next to each fund based on how it performed in the past month. That's all. That was her whole system and it turned 19 grand into 48 grand in 29 months. Turn the page for the statements.

In February 2000, Sharlene was 27 years old and made less than $30,000 per year. She never watched the stock market. She doesn't even like the stock market, and she never once looked at

Charles Schwab — Statement

ACCOUNT NUMBER / TAX ID NUMBER	PERIOD COVERED	LAST STATEMENT	PAGE
	SEP 1 - SEP 30 1997		1

BROKERAGE ACCOUNT

TITLE OF ACCOUNT

OFFICE SERVING YOUR ACCOUNT

SHARLENE CHOY

BRANCH HOURS: 8AM-5PM M-F

*** FOR QUESTIONS ABOUT THIS STATEMENT: CALL 1-800-435-4000   *** ACCOUNT OPENED IN: 1997

STATUS OF KEY VALUES AS OF SEP 30 1997

		ACCOUNT TRANSACTION SUMMARY	
Investments Owned	$7,568.03	OPENING CASH BALANCE	$.00
Net Portfolio Value	$7,568.03	Funds Received	$1,000.00
Ending Cash Balance	$.00	Total Credits	$7,500.00
TOTAL ACCOUNT VALUE	$7,568.03	Investment Purchases	($7,500.00)
Total Funds Available	$.00	MoneyFund Purch/Reinvest	($1,000.00)
		Total Debits	($8,500.00)
		ENDING CASH BALANCE	$.00

RATE SUMMARY AS OF 09/30

MMF Yield*	CAF Yield*	GSF Yield*	TEF Yield*	STF Yield*	Margin Loan Rate
4.98%	3.20%	4.87%	3.35%	4.75%	7.75% to 9.25%

* 7 Day Annualized Yield. Please see reverse for more information.

PORTFOLIO POSITION DETAIL

CATEGORY	S LONG/ SHORT	QUOTE SYMBOL	QUANTITY	LATEST PRICE	MARKET VALUE
MUTUAL FUNDS	C Long	JAOSX	132.626	19.0700	$2,529.18
	C Long	OAKLX	155.376	16.3400	$2,538.84
	C Long	PBTCX	113.792	21.9700	$2,500.01

Net Portfolio Value $7,568.03

ACCOUNT TRANSACTION DETAIL

DATE	TRANSACTION	QUANTITY	DESCRIPTION	PRICE	AMOUNT
			Opening Cash Balance		$.00
09/15	Funds Received		FUNDS RECEIVED *		$1,000.00
09/15	Bought		SCHWAB MONEY MARKET FUND	1.0000	($1,000.00)
09/24	Funds Received		FUNDS RECEIVED *		$1,000.00
09/25	Bought	132.626	JANUS OVERSEAS FUND	18.8500	($2,500.00)
09/25	Bought	155.376	OAKMARK SELECT FUND	16.0900	($2,500.00)
09/25	Bought	113.792	PBHG TECHNOLOGY & COMMS	21.9700	($2,500.00)
09/26	Redeemed	09/26	SCHWAB MONEY MARKET FUND	1.0000	$1,000.00
			Ending Cash Balance		$.00

*** CONTINUED ON NEXT PAGE ***

SEE REVERSE SIDE FOR STATEMENT INFORMATION

© Charles Schwab & Co., Inc.   Member: New York Stock Exchange, Inc. and other principal stock and option exchanges.

Charles Schwab — Statement

ACCOUNT NUMBER	PERIOD COVERED	LAST STATEMENT	PAGE
	FEB 1 - FEB 29 2000	JAN 2000	1

BROKERAGE ACCOUNT

TITLE OF ACCOUNT

OFFICE SERVING YOUR ACCOUNT

SHARLENE CHOY

*ASK ABOUT OUR WEB WORKSHOPS

*** FOR QUESTIONS ABOUT THIS STATEMENT: CALL 1-800-435-4000   *** ACCOUNT OPENED IN: 1997

STATUS OF KEY VALUES AS OF FEB 29 2000

		ACCOUNT TRANSACTION SUMMARY	
Investments Owned	$48,199.23	OPENING CASH BALANCE	$1.54
Net Portfolio Value	$48,199.23	Investment Sales	$11,632.63
Ending Cash Balance	$195.97	Funds Received	$3,300.00
TOTAL ACCOUNT VALUE	$48,395.20	Total Credits	$14,932.63
Change in Value from 01/00	$14,031.39	Investment Purchases	($14,932.20)
		Total Debits	($14,932.20)
Total Funds Available	$195.97	ENDING CASH BALANCE	$195.97

RATE SUMMARY AS OF 02/29

MMF Yield*	CAF Yield*	GSF Yield*	TEF Yield*	STF Yield*	Margin Loan Rate
5.27%	2.34%	5.14%	3.14%	4.86%	8.37% to 9.87%

* 7 Day Annualized Yield. Please see reverse for more information.

PORTFOLIO POSITION DETAIL

CATEGORY	S LONG/ SHORT	QUOTE SYMBOL	QUANTITY	LATEST PRICE	MARKET VALUE
MUTUAL FUNDS	C Long	JAOSX	208.034	63.6000	$13,230.96
	C Long	JAOSX	269.929	44.9300	$12,127.91
	C Long	JAGLX	150.602	26.8500	$4,043.66
	C Long	PBTCX	189.292	99.3000	$18,796.70

Net Portfolio Value $48,199.23

ACCOUNT TRANSACTION DETAIL

DATE	TRANSACTION	QUANTITY	DESCRIPTION	PRICE	AMOUNT
			Opening Cash Balance		$1.54
02/03	Funds Received		FUNDS RECEIVED *		$3,400.00
02/03	Bought	113.516	JANUS OLYMPUS FUND	26.6500	($3,408.00)
02/03	Bought	150.602	JANUS GLOBAL LIFE SCIENC FUND	26.8300	($3,000.00)
02/04	Sold	368.332-	OAKMARK SELECT FUND	17.6700	$6,502.43
02/04	Sold	70-	PBHG TECHNOLOGY & COMMS	76.0600	$5,324.20
02/07	Bought	94.518	JANUS OLYMPUS FUND		($5,324.20)
02/15	MoneyLink Txn		AUTHORIZED TRANSFER From # 9101329905		$300.00
02/23	Bought	2.364	JANUS OVERSEAS FUND	42.3000	($100.00)

*** CONTINUED ON NEXT PAGE ***

SEE REVERSE SIDE FOR STATEMENT INFORMATION

© Charles Schwab & Co., Inc.   Member: New York Stock Exchange, Inc. and other principal stock and option exchanges.

which stocks her mutual funds owned. Yet she ended up with almost 50 grand in a Schwab account. During the 2000–2001 bear market, PBHG Tech fell 72 percent and Sharlene's Schwab account dipped to an April 2001 balance of $20,780. She kept buying each month at lower prices. When the rubber band snaps back in the other direction she'll make a profit.

Notice that even after the worst bear market in Nasdaq history, Sharlene didn't lose any of her investment principal. She lost almost all of her gains, but none of her principal. That's doing pretty well in my book (which you happen to be reading at the moment, so we'll go with that angle). By selling at the peak, Sharlene could have kept the $27,419 she lost when her portfolio dropped 57 percent, but come on. Coulda, woulda, shoulda is an easy game to play, looking back. Nobody gets it right looking forward. As of April 2001, Sharlene was able to invest her new money at cheap prices. As the years tick by, her diligence will pay off handsomely.

Is there any reason you can't do that? Nope. Do you think anybody can get ahead over time? You bet. And in the collective experience of everyone I've met in the world of stocks and bonds and mutual funds, that's what it means to be a do-it-yourself investor. It's not about inside information. It's not about weekend conferences at resort islands. It's not about daytrading.

What it *is* about is finding investments that will perform well over the long haul and buying more of them every month during that long haul. One of the surest bets is the U.S. stock market as captured by Vanguard's S&P 500 index fund. It's about as prudent and reliable and boring as an investment can be, but the darned thing works over time, and it's cheap. You won't appreciate the power of working over time and being cheap until you've dabbled where nothing works, everything is expensive, and you just wish you had your money back. Avoid that. Reread "The Simplest Investment Plan Ever" on page 116 and start this month.

Too stodgy, you say? All right, here's something better. I'm building commercial property that floats around the Pacific and rents out daytrading terminals for a cut of the profits. Forget about annual performance, this is guaranteed to double your money every three months. A full unit is $20,000 but since you're one of my readers I'll let you in for $5,000. Call me.

APPENDIX 1

The View from My Piece Of Flotsam

I tried keeping this book current with changing market conditions, but finally gave up. The market, as you must surely realize by now, never stops changing. For me to postpone publication until the bear market is officially over flies in the face of this book's claim to show you time-tested principles for making money in any market. That's why I will immediately put my money where my mouth is. Or at least where my keyboard is.

Today is Wednesday, June 27, 2001. Time for the book to go to New York for layout and publication. That means I can't add any more to it after today. So I'm going to take a look at the market as it stands now to show you how uncertain things remain at this very moment. I will then pick seven investments that you can monitor from here to eternity to see just how well the principles you discovered in this book hold up. You might be reading these words in January 2002 or June 2005 or at any other point in the future. Checking up on these picks will be interesting, I'm sure.

Dateline: June 27, 2001

Today the Federal Reserve has cut interest rates by 25 basis points. A basis point is one one hundreth of a percent, so 25 basis points is 0.25 percent, also called a quarter of a point. These things are important to know as you cull through the daily haul of financial reporting. After this, the sixth cut so far in 2001, the federal funds rate stands at 3.75 percent. Since the first cut in January, the Fed has lowered interest rates by 2.75 percent. That's a lot.

One side of the financial community says this is dire news because only if the economy is in serious trouble—and we all know it is—will the Fed be moving so aggressively. The other side of the financial communitys says this is fabulous news because if the economy is about to recover—and we all know it is—the aggressiveness of the Fed will move things along in fine fashion. *Stay on the sidelines,* says the first group. If you do anything, short stocks so you make money as they sink lower and the United States becomes irrelevant as an economic power. *Dive in,* says the second group. Take out a second mortgage on your house to buy stocks at these bargain prices. Don't just borrow money from your mortgage lender, go on margin to also borrow money from your broker. Now is the time to show conviction.

I hasten to remind you that the evidence of the past year favors the first group. The Nasdaq closed today at 2075, some 60 percent below its close on March 10, 2000. So far in 2001, it's down 16 percent. These are not happy days in the market and the experts have wasted no time in telling us that. One analyst has written that the longer-term impact of cutting rates is negative because the Fed is running out of fixes to stimulate the stagnating economy. Another writes that the government is doing its best to not have a stock market collapse. He went on to warn that if the Dow and S&P 500 collapse like the Nasdaq has done, Americans will dramatically reduce their participation in the economy. An investment strategist has said he believes the economic numbers and earnings will deteriorate for months to come.

The recent earnings picture has been bleak. Applied Micro Circuits lowered its fiscal first-quarter outlook to a loss from a profit because of market weakness. Tellabs Chairman Michael Birck has told Reuters that "the telephone companies have basically stopped buying. They have turned off the spigot." Level 3 Communications has warned of weak revenue and cash flow for the next two years. Oracle has managed to beat analysts' estimates by a penny but did so by dramatically decreasing costs, not by increasing sales. And so on. The current situation is ugly. Most people, analysts included, think that their money should be anywhere *but* the stock market.

Friends, from what you read in this book and what you instinctively know about the way the world works, doesn't this seem like a pretty good time to be buying? It does to me. Then again, it should never be about market timing, right? The question is not whether June 2001 is a good time to buy. The question is always, Do I intend to leave this money in the market for the long term? If so, then it's always a good time to buy. I am personally in the market as I write this. Many of my own investments have lost money in the past year. I am not selling; I am buying more. I am doing so because I believe in the companies, I'm in for the long term, and I believe that this is a good buying opportunity just like every other month in a long-term investment program. June 2001 just happens to be a much better opportunity than I found in June 2000.

Kelly's Heroes: Stocking Up Your Recovery Portfolio

The Nasdaq ship has sunk, and I'm left floating on a piece of flotsam in a roiling sea. Where to put my new money? Which parts of the ship will float again and one day sail toward the sun? These are questions I am really asking at the moment, and they are questions you will ask many times as a do-it-yourself investor.

As for me, I'm going with the S&P 500 index and quality technology companies at cheap prices. I believe in buying things on sale, and at the moment, nothing is as bargain-priced as technology. I don't care how much the sharp-penciled analysts howl at me for buying stocks that are down more than 60 percent, I'm doing it. Here's my recovery portfolio:

KELLY'S HEROES: STOCKING UP YOUR RECOVERY PORTFOLIO

% of Portfolio	Investment	6/27/2001 Close	Off 52-Wk High
10	Cable & Wireless (CWP)	$16.16	−74%
10	Cisco Systems (CSCO)	$17.93	−74%
10	DSP Group (DSPG)	$19.50	−70%
10	Exar (EXAR)	$17.84	−72%
40	iShares S&P 500 Index (IVV)	$121.31	−21%
10	Oracle (ORCL)	$18.04	−61%
10	Tellabs (TLAB)	$10.03	−78%

I need to deviate from real life a bit because once the book is printed I can't change anything. The book can only buy at these prices and be done. In real life, however, I am not moving 100 percent of my cash into these positions on June 27, 2001, for all the reasons you read in "Wade In, Don't Dive" on page 108. Cisco might be cheap at $17.93, but it might get cheaper. In fact, just a week ago I could have bought in for $16.40. However, three weeks ago I would have paid $20.76. This constant fluctuation is the reason I buy and sell gradually in real life. I can't do that on these pages.

Where did I go to find the companies in the recovery portfolio? Why, my newsletter, *The NeatSheet,* of course! I use the resources you learned about in this book to gather ideas for the newsletter. *Worth* ran an excellent article about Oracle. *SmartMoney* touted Exar in a column about value investing. I saw in *Investor's Business Daily* that a mutual fund I respect is buying shares of Cable & Wireless. I checked each company's recent filings on the Internet at 10-K Wizard and read profiles at Yahoo Finance. I researched competitors with Power Investor software. When it came time to buy, I did so online at Ameritrade.

Notice that I did not use Vanguard's index fund to tap the S&P 500. The Vanguard fund is the core of my strategy called "The Simplest Investment Plan Ever," page 116. Why then would I not use it here in my recovery portfolio? Because Vanguard funds are only available with a Vanguard account. I could not buy into the fund at Ameritrade. I could, however, buy what's called an iShare.

An iShare is an *exchange-traded fund*, or ETF. It's just like a mutual fund in the sense that it's a pool of investments managed by a professional. Unlike a regular mutual fund, however, you buy and sell shares of ETFs just like shares of stock. You can buy them through any broker, get in and out at any time, place limit orders, everything. And get this: ETFs charge lower expenses than their mutual fund counterparts. The iShare S&P 500 Index Fund, for instance, costs only 0.09 percent per year as compared to the Vanguard S&P 500 index fund at 0.20 percent. You do pay brokerage fees to buy and sell iShares, just like any stock, but doing so online keeps those costs minimal. At Ameritrade it's only $8 per market order.

Are iShares superior to the Vanguard S&P 500 index fund for "The Simplest Investment Plan Ever"? No, because they require a little extra work. You have to actually buy shares each month. With an account at Vanguard, you can set up an automatic transfer from your bank account that goes directly into the fund. Set up the program and forget about it, and in twenty years you can come back to see what happened. With iShares, you have to buy each month, even if you automatically transfer the money from your bank account. Buying is a small effort, but you know as well as I do that a lot of people would forget to do it month after month. After twenty years of fits and starts, they probably would have ended up with more money by automating the process at Vanguard.

Back to my recovery portfolio. It is heavily weighted toward technology, and in many schools of thought, that's a sin. But the time-tested principles you have discovered in this book suggest that buying bargains is the way to wealth. The 2000–2001 bear market has placed technology on sale, so that's what I'm buying.

Each of the six stocks earns money. That's nice to know. Each of them has been unduly punished (in my opinion) by the widespread collapse caused by the Internet bubble. Each of them will one day look good again. I made a lot of money with this same technique applied to IBM in 1993, when the company was considering a breakup into twenty separate operating units. The stock fell and the news was dire, but I bought more shares every two weeks for four years. IBM is now once again considered a strong company, worthy of widow and orphan money. Buying during its darkest hour proved very profitable. I think it will be the same with these six stocks.

My recovery portfolio is tied to the times because it's buying what's on sale today, June 27, 2001. It's possible that a copy of this book will be shrink wrapped and buried with White House evidence files until the year 2276, when an archaeology student digs them up and rewrites history. The companies I chose might look downright dated by then. Some won't even exist. So to make this book timeless as a service to archaeologists blowing dirt from these pages, let's look at two portfolios designed not for June 27, 2001, but for any date.

Good for All Eons

The best place to find companies that will do business with your great-great-grandchildren is the Dow Jones Industrial Average. The thirty companies are such powerhouses that whatever risks you encounter among them are risks you face with any stocks. It is nearly impossible to be an irresponsible investor when restricting yourself to Dow companies.

One of the best ways to determine which Dow stocks to buy is by looking at their dividend yields. A high dividend yield usually means a bargain-price stock. This strategy is explained completely in Chapter 4 of *The Neatest Little Guide to Stock Market Investing*. The idea is to switch every twelve months from last year's cheap Dow stocks to this year's. Because Dow Dividend strategies involve switching every year, they are not suitable plans for creating a portfolio good for all eons. But for you, a person alive and well in this eon, they are a swell way to prosper in good times and bad. I suggest that you learn about the Dow Dividend strategies and consider spending the required fifteen minutes per year to maintain one of them.

Now, about that strategy good for all eons: I have two approaches. My first approach is to invest in twelve Dow leaders and the S&P MidCap 400 stock index. My second approach is to invest in the S&P 500 and the S&P MidCap 400 in equal amounts. Let's have a look at both approaches.

Dow/MidCap Portfolio

Here's my first portfolio good for all eons, hereafter called the Dow/MidCap portfolio:

% of Portfolio	Investment	6/27/2001 Close	Off 52-Wk High
5	AT&T (T)	$20.7	−41%
5	Boeing (BA)	$57.70	−19%
5	Citigroup (C)	$51.70	−13%
5	Coca-Cola (KO)	$44.18	−31%
5	ExxonMobil (XOM)	$87.22	−9%
5	General Electric (GE)	$48.26	−20%
5	Home Depot (HD)	$46.85	−22%
40	iShares S&P MidCap 400 Index (IJH)	$101.45	−8%
5	Int'l Business Machines (IBM)	$113.52	−16%
5	McDonald's (MCD)	$27.51	−22%
5	Merck (MRK)	$65.64	−32%
5	Microsoft (MSFT)	$71.14	−13%
5	Wal-Mart (WMT)	$48.50	−20%

That's quite a swath of American business, wouldn't you say? It covers telecommunications, aerospace, finance, food, energy, electronics, retailing, computer hardware and software, and healthcare. As long as people keep communicating, flying, banking, eating, turning on lights, buying things, getting sick, and sending e-mail, the portfolio should be fine.

You might wonder why I've suddenly abandoned the trusty S&P 500 index for its brother, the S&P MidCap 400 index. The reason is that the 500 covers the largest companies in America. Notice that the Dow covers the same group and that the twelve stocks in the portfolio are lumbering giants of business. Putting the 40 percent index money into the S&P 500 would be redundant. Putting it into the next tier of business, the mid cap companies, provides smarter diversification. Not only that, but the S&P MidCap 400 index has performed better than the 500 in all time frames over the past ten years. Compare the two:

S&P 500 05/31/01		S&P MidCap 400 05/31/01	
Year-to-Date	−4.37%	Year-to Date	1.38%
1 Year	−10.55%	1 Year	10.92%
3-Year Avg	6.15%	3-Year Avg	14.07%
5-Year Avg	15.13%	5-Year Avg	18.27%
10-Year Avg	14.83%	10-Year Avg	17.03%

As you can see, those mid cap companies are good to have on your side. They form the sweet spot of the stock market, not as crash-happy as small upstarts but not as established and slow-moving as large companies. For the past ten years the mid caps have been just right. Balanced against the 60 percent of this portfolio invested in Dow companies, the mid cap index is a perfect fit.

If you're still bright-eyed and bushy-tailed after implementing the Dow/MidCap portfolio and would like to improve its performance just a tad, I suggest rebalancing annually. That will keep the percentages in line and force you to sell high and buy low. For example, if AT&T stages a dramatic recovery to $80 while ExxonMobil falls to $20, the percentage of your portfolio in AT&T would be too big and your percentage in ExxonMobil would be too small. To get back to 5 percent in each, you would sell the appropriate amount of AT&T and buy the appropriate amount of ExxonMobil. Do this every year across the entire portfolio to return it to its original allocations and you should make money through several presidents, wars, scandals, weather anomalies, pop music hits, strange fashion fads, and belt sizes.

Of course, if you're going to be involved with your portfolio enough each year to rebalance it, you'll be involved enough to implement the aforementioned Dow Dividend strategies. Again, they're worth knowing about. But if fifteen minutes of work per year exceeds your threshold, then let this Dow/MidCap portfolio ride out fluctuations on its own. The market will rebalance your allocations over time. You'll just miss the annual chance to sell high and buy low.

While my Dow/MidCap portfolio is a prudent approach to long-term investing, it's not quite as bulletproof as my next portfolio.

Kevlar 500/400 Portfolio

Here's my second portfolio good for all eons, hereafter called the bullet-proof Kevlar 500/400 portfolio, or just K54:

% of Portfolio	Investment	6/27/2001 Close	Off 52-Wk High
50	iShares S&P 500 Index (IVV)	$121.31	−21%
50	iShares S&P MidCap 400 Index (IJH)	$101.45	−8%

After starting K54, you could freeze yourself in liquid nitrogen for three generations and thaw out to find that your money had become a fortune. There would be no catastrophes. Believe me, if the S&P 500 and the S&P MidCap 400 had gone belly up, there was nowhere to hide.

K54 will probably outperform "The Simplest Investment Plan Ever" on page 116. It might be cheaper, too. The annual expense ratios of iShare funds are lower than Vanguard funds. You do, however, pay brokerage commissions every time you buy and sell iShares because they are treated just like stocks. You could invest larger sums less frequently to offset the bokerage commissions— for example, quarterly instead of monthly—but all-in-all the expense issue when comparing iShares and Vanguard funds is probably a wash. iShares are cheaper for lump-sum investors, and Vanguard is cheaper for monthly investors.

The reason I still tip my hat to the Vanguard strategy is that it allows you to automate your monthly investments. Unflagging devotion to a regular investment schedule is extremely effective, much better than hot tips and winning systems. The power of "The Simplest Investment Plan Ever" is its simplicity. People will actually do it. There is no need to remember to buy, no need to research dividend yields, no need to rebalance, no need to do much of anything except exist and make sure there's money in your bank account for the monthly transfer.

If you would like to improve "The Simplest Investment Plan Ever" just a bit, then tell Vanguard to put half of your monthly investment into its S&P 500 fund (VFINX) and half into its S&P MidCap 400 fund (VIMSX). You will tap the potentially higher return of the MidCap 400, the plan is still automated, and you're still free to have another beer.

To learn more about the companies I've chosen and to see how my three portfolios are doing, visit **www.jasonkelly.com/doityourself.html**.

APPENDIX 2:

Your Risk Rundown

Risk, risk, risk. It's all you heard about in the aftermath of the 2000–2001 bear market. During the bull run of the 1990s, people weren't as concerned with risk. More than any article or book you'll ever read, losing 68 percent of your portfolio will convince you of the need to manage risk.

Here is a little questionnaire I've developed to help you understand your own risk tolerance. It's not the most scientific approach ever taken, but it'll help you decide if your disposition toward investing is conservative, moderate, or aggressive.

- How much car insurance do you buy?
  (A) The most I can afford.
  (B) Only what's legally required.
  (C) None. I don't care what the law says.

- How much time will the money you invest stay invested?
  (A) Less than two years.
  (B) Two to ten years.
  (C) More than ten years.

- When hearing the phrase "You can't lose," you think:
  (A) I probably *will* lose.
  (B) I wonder if that could be true?
  (C) Well, heck, let's get started then!

- You're on vacation in Hawaii. You turn on the radio looking for music and hear "Today the Nasdaq plunged 4.8 percent on heavy volume as earnings —" You:
  (A) Feel little explosions along your spinal column as you yell for everyone to shut up so you can hear the rest of the report.
  (B) Keep looking for music but wonder how your portfolio is holding up.
  (C) Find the music, turn it up, and don't give a second thought to the Nasdaq.

- Describe the stability of your income:
  (A) I run to the mailbox every day hoping to find a check—very unstable.
  (B) I like my current occupation and expect to continue—somewhat stable.
  (C) I've been in my career for years without interruption—very stable.

- In the 2000–2001 bear market, the Nasdaq lost 68 percent and the S&P 500 lost 27 percent. If you owned an S&P 500 index fund during that time, you would have:
  (A) Sold after losing 15 percent.
  (B) Held on tight through it all, knowing that it would one day recover.
  (C) Kept on buying as the price sank lower and lower each month, knowing that you would make money on the recovery instead of just getting back to even.

Give yourself one point for every A, two for every B, and three for every C, then find your score below:

6–9 points: You're a conservative investor. You should look toward dividing your money evenly among stocks, bonds, and money market mutual funds. For the stock portion of your portfolio, you should strongly consider investing in the S&P 500, either through an index mutual fund or Spiders (see page 148). Individual stock fluctuations might lead you to drink or pull your hair out or otherwise become an unpleasant person.

10–13 points: You're a moderate investor. You should put about half your money in the S&P 500 and divide the other half between some high-quality stocks or conservative stock mutual funds and a bond fund. By high-quality stocks I mean the kind you find on the Dow: large, well established, well run, and likely one day to do business with your grandchildren. Such companies are household names and will not be hard for you to research. In fact, start with the companies on the Dow. Surely you can find something you want among the likes of AT&T, Boeing, Coca-Cola, Disney, General Electric, Home Depot, IBM, Intel, McDonald's, Microsoft, and Wal-Mart. It's hard to go too far afield when choosing investments from the list of 30 Dow stocks.

14–18 points: You're an aggressive investor. You should put all your money in stocks. I still think the S&P 500 is a good idea, but you'll probably want to complement it with individual stocks that you choose. A good balance is to put 40 or 50 percent of your money in the S&P 500 and the remainder in your own stock picks. A smart progression is to go from the S&P 500 to Dow stocks to lesser-known stocks with greater potential—and greater risk. I like the ramp-up strategy. Remember from "Wade In, Don't Dive" (page 108) that you should move gradually. Working your way from safe, moderate-return stocks to risky, high-return stocks is one way to do so.

This rough guideline will help you get the big pieces of your portfolio in place. Don't overdo the planning, though. The most important factor is the amount of time your money will be invested. If it's for more than ten years, get in the stock market, invest every month, and quit watching.

APPENDIX 3:

Fill Your 401(k)

Retirement is in your hands, one way or another. You cannot depend on Social Security because the money you pay into the program today is not being saved or invested for you. It's being spent on the current generation of retirees. When you retire, your payout will come from the paychecks of people working at that time. The size of that workforce is due to shrink as compared to the number of retirees drawing from Social Security. Translation: you won't be drinking a Mai Tai on Mallorca courtesy of the Social Security program. You'll be lucky to get a jar of peanuts. Don't panic, because there are lots of ways to add more money to your retirement kitty. In fact, I suggest you assume that Social Security will provide you with nothing. If it does trickle a few dollars in your direction, consider it a nice little bonus.

The simplest and best way to plan for retirement is by participating in your company's 401(k) plan. If you work for a nonprofit organization, it's called a 403(b) plan but works the same way. The plans are not only easy to use because they take your contributions straight out of your paycheck, but they can also give you free cash. Many employers and organizations will match every dollar you contribute with 10 cents, 25 cents, or 50 cents extra. Plus, your contribution to the pot is taken from your paycheck before you pay income taxes and it grows tax-free until you begin withdrawing in retirement. That means you put your $1.00 into the plan before the government turns it into 72 cents. If your company also matches 25 cents, you just put $1.25 away for retirement while in effect spending only 72 cents out of pocket. That's an immediate 74 percent return on your investment. If you can't see the wisdom in that, nothing I write will ever help you.

Here's a simple two-step plan for your 401(k) or 403(b):

1. Contribute the maximum amount.
2. Put your entire account in the stock market index fund.

If your plan allows you to contribute up to 10 percent of your paycheck, contribute the full 10 percent. If it allows you to contribute up to 15 percent, contribute the full 15 percent. You will soon get used to living on less and won't even know you're doing it because the "extra" money won't ever show up in your bank account. There was a time in your life when you managed to live on 15 percent less than you make today. There are other people doing it right now. Don't be a fool. Take advantage of the tax savings, convenience, and potential free money that are yours in a 401(k) or 403(b).

Almost all 401(k) and 403(b) plans offer a stock market index fund as one of several places you can invest. The index might be the S&P 500 or Wilshire 5000 or some other broad-based market index. Choose it for 100 percent of your account. This piece of advice rankles my prudent peers who say your account should be diversified, but I don't care. The S&P 500 is not Las Vegas or pets.com or a pyramid scheme. It's the collective potential of the U.S. economy and it has proven to be the best long-term investment out there. It is not a foolhardy choice. It will fluctuate, as you know by now, but your automatic regular contributions will take advantage of that fluctuation by buying more shares when the price is down and fewer when it's up. (See "Keep Investing—The Advantage of Dollar-Cost Averaging" on page 105.) Your retirement account is nearly guaranteed to have a long enough time frame to be safely invested in the stock market because your retirement age is not when the fat lady sings. Life expectancy is increasing every year. Many of today's retirees live another 25 or 30 years after they stop working. As every valedictorian will say in her trite graduation speech, "It's not the end; it's just the beginning."

Don't put too much money in your company's stock. An automatic benefit of choosing the stock market index fund in Step 2 is that you diversify your financial health beyond your employer. You already work at the company, so all your money comes from the company's good fortune. If that fortune disappears, your income might too. You don't want to be looking for another job while your retirement account sinks with the company stock price. Do your best for the company, keep your income rising, but invest your retirement in the overall U.S. stock market.

There's a lot more to be said about retirement planning, but not in this book. If you want to know more about it from me, visit **www.jasonkelly.com/retirement.html**.

APPENDIX 4:

Why I Detest Analysts

Any author who writes a book about investing with "do-it-yourself" in the title has to detest analysts. It's a requirement. I thought I should at least pay them the respect of explaining why I detest them and why I encourage you to detest them as well.

There's a lot to detest. Merrill Lynch ran a two-page ad in April 2001 with the headline "Techtelligence." It explained that the firm employs 100 analysts who've won awards for their coverage of 500 companies. Further, the ad bragged about Merrill offering "the top tier in research." When you know Merrill's track record in the tech investment business, you'll wonder what qualifies as bottom tier.

The firm took twenty Internet companies public in the four years preceding the ad. When the ad ran, two of the companies were already bankrupt, eight were down more than 90 percent, and fifteen traded below their stock's initial public offering price. That's some bangup, top-tier performance. I'm sure you can't wait to start following every word from those 100 analysts.

Just who were Merrill's companies? Pets.com was one of them. In ten months it went from a $66 million IPO to six feet under. 24/7 Media is another. It began its public life in August 1998 at $18.50 per share. It reached $65 in January 2000 and on April 4, 2001, it hit $0.19. It has yet to earn its first dollar. Let's see how well Merrill's "Techtelligence" guided investors through that frenetic history.

The company initiated coverage on 24/7 Media with a near-term accumulate / long-term buy rating. The stock did well that first year and started August 1999 at $30.56. Merrill upgraded the near-term accumulate to near-term buy, and by the end of the month the price was $34.25. The price shot to $65 in January, then skidded to $11.75 in August 2000. That's when Merrill decided to downgrade both near-term and long-term ratings from buy to accumulate. As of this writing in June 2001, the firm still suggests that investors accumulate shares at the bargain price of $0.31. Merrill's advice lost 98 percent from the IPO, lost 99 percent from August 1999, and lost 97 percent from August 2000.

Merrill Lynch's offering and coverage of 24/7 Media would be an unfair example if it were an isolated incident, but it's not. During the period of January 1997 through April 2001, here's how four top investment banks performed:

Firm	Number of IPOs	Average Performance
Goldman Sachs	47	−16%
Credit Suisse First Boston	75	−41%
Robertson Stephens	38	−65%
Merrill Lynch	20	−82%

One excuse provided for the abysmal performance was that the market was demanding new high-tech firms to buy and the investment bankers had no choice but to deliver them. Here you thought the analysts were supposed to guide you to the right investments but came to find out that they just give you what you want. Evidently, you wanted companies with no viable business model or earnings.

Merrill Lynch posted billboards near my home in Los Angeles with the advice to "Be Bullish." It's good advice if you're in the market for the long term and are buying quality companies at reasonable prices. But it's hard to imagine that's what Merrill had in mind. We can be forgiven for remembering that Merrill was bullish all the way down on stocks that went bankrupt or lost more than 90 percent of their value. Merrill's logo is a bull. I see it devouring investor money at the front and excreting investor returns at the back.

Speaking of money, the investment bankers make a lot of it even when they give bad advice. While investors lost big time, Merrill pocketed an average $105 million for each of its IPOs. Robertson Stephens averaged $61 million. Credit Suisse First Boston, $73 million. Goldman Sachs, $121 million. Detect a pattern?

Yes, the rumors are true. There is a conflict of interest in the investment advice business. As you have read in "Brother-in-Law Brokers" on page 89, analysts do not have your best interests in mind. They advise you on whether to buy or sell a product that they hope you buy from them. It's like asking a Ford dealer whether you should buy the new Ford pickup. What do you think he'll say? No? "Buy the Chevy"? "I wouldn't if I were you"?

You can gather just about all you need to know about the analyst advice business by looking over the Securities Industry Association's list of "best practices." The list was prepared by fourteen of Wall Street's biggest firms in advance of an investigation by the Securities and Exchange Commission, the regulatory division of the National Association of Securities Dealers, and the U.S. attorney's office in New York. Among other pointers that are self-evident to even the most casual system of ethics, the list recommended that analysts:

- Use "the full ratings spectrum" including "sell" when rating a stock.

- Should receive compensation based on the outcome of their advice.

- Should not "trade against" their own advice by, for instance, selling what they just told you to buy.

We can assume that before this list was circulated, analysts were free to never issue a "sell" rating, were compensated whether you made money or not, and routinely did the exact opposite of what they told you to do. Great bunch of folks to have on your side.

Join me in detesting analysts. It's good to buy stocks. It's good to be bullish. But do it yourself so that you can be profitable too.

APPENDIX 5:

Do-It-Yourself Investor Tools

Here's a recap of what you read in this book and a listing of all the tools to get you started. Chapters 1 and 7 don't include tools so this collection covers only Chapters 2 through 6.

This Book as a Brochure

If I had to condense this entire book into a brochure for people to read while stuck in traffic, what follows is what it would look like.

Chapter 2: Opportunity and Risk in Stocks

- Keep your money in stocks because they return more than other investments. There are no guarantees, but the market has averaged about 11 percent a year since 1926.

- Bear markets like the one spanning 2000–2001, when the Nasdaq lost 68 percent, show you that the stock market can give a rough ride over the short term. It's best for your long-term money.

- Don't waste your time looking for The Winning System because it doesn't exist. Promises of super-high returns in short periods are lies. Buy quality companies, and be patient.
- Be careful of stock market fraud. Don't fall prey to Internet pump-and-dump. Anything that sounds outrageous is.
- Skip real estate investments because they're a lot of work and usually end up returning less than what you'd have made in the stock market anyway.
- Avoid limited partnerships because they almost always lose money.
- Don't put your money in lending investments, like bank accounts or bonds. You'll never get ahead moving that slowly.
- Don't get flimflammed by everyday money fraud, like prime bank securities or pyramid schemes. It's embarrassing.

Chapter 3: The Calm Investor

- Nobody can predict the direction of the market. None of the analysts, none of the media, none of your colleagues, not you, not me, nobody.
- Greed and fear are the primary emotions of investing. Learn about these two tricksters and get them under control before they attack.
- Know in advance that you hate losing more than you love winning. You'll feel like garbage when the market goes down but feel only mild contentment when it goes up.
- Also, you'd rather get ahead than be ahead. Your financial happiness has more to do with the direction your wealth is taking than your actual worth.
- Give up trying to guess the market. Most of the annual gains happen on just three days per year.

- Resign yourself to losing money now and then, because you will.

Chapter 4:
In the Oysters and Under the Rocks

- Think like an investor by always looking for an opportunity to put your money to work.
- When you're first starting out, absorb everything. Read every business and investment publication you can get your hands on.
- After a time, you'll tire of absorbing everything and focus on the good stuff.
- Learn what to ignore. Half of being an informed investor is knowing which information you don't need.
- Don't let investment software sucker you into daytrading. If anything, use software databases to research long-term holdings.
- Copy successful professionals. Read mutual fund reports to see what stocks your favorite managers like. Read *Investor's Business Daily* to see what top funds are buying and selling.

Chapter 5:
The Path to the Simplest Investment Plan Ever

- Avoid full-service brokers because the full service they provide is laughable.
- Get an online discount broker because you'll save up to 99 percent off the full-service price.

- Understand the pros and cons of market and limit orders, then choose an approach that fits your style.

- Choose the best investments, then concentrate your money on those. Owning a little of everything will lead to crummy performance.

- Keep investing no matter what. Your regular contributions will buy more when prices are low and less when prices are high. It's like magic.

- Invest gradually because the day will come when you're wrong about a stock's future, and you'll be glad you didn't shoot your whole wad of cash.

- Learn gradually. When you're just starting out, manage only a portion of your money and that in mutual funds.

- The simplest investment plan is to send money every month to the Vanguard S&P 500 index fund. You'll match the market's performance, pay almost nothing in fees, and your tax bill will be low.

Chapter 6: Finding $500 per Month

- Your best bet for big savings is your housing payment, whether mortgage or rent. Get creative in finding an affordable place to live. They're out there.

- Driving a used car can mean the difference between being permanently in debt or permanently ahead. Look in the newspaper.

- Save in the grocery store by getting items on sale and cheaper brands.

- Make your long-distance phone calls through OneSuite.com. It's only 2.9 cents per minute in the forty-eight states.

- Pay off your credit cards.

- Take the highest possible deductible on your insurance

policies because the chance of ever needing to use your insurance is low. That's why they insure you in the first place.

- If you need life insurance, get term. It's cheap, and you buy only what you need. If you don't have any human dependents, you don't need any life insurance.
- You can always take a second job for extra money, but make it something you enjoy. Turn your recreation to income.
- Starting your own business can be the most fulfilling way of all to make a few bucks. You get to choose exactly what to do, you make money, you get tax benefits, and you have access to good retirement programs.

Resources from This Book

Books

Investment Psychology Explained: Classic Strategies to Beat the Markets by Martin J. Pring (1992), page 54.

Mind Over Money: Match Your Personality to a Winning Financial Strategy by John W. Schott (1998), pages 54–55.

Profits Without Panic: Investment Psychology for Personal Wealth by Jonathan Myers (1999), page 55.

Why Smart People Make Big Money Mistakes—and How to Correct Them: Lessons from the New Science of Behavioral Economics by Gary Belsky and Thomas Gilovich (1999), page 55.

Brokers

Ameritrade: www.ameritrade.com, page 118.

E*Trade: www.etrade.com, page 119.

Fidelity: (800) 343-3548, www.fidelity.com, page 119.

National Discount Brokers: www.ndb.com, page 119.

Schwab: (800) 435-4000, www.schwab.com, page 119.

Vanguard: (800) 871-3879, www.vanguard.com, page 119.

Insurance

Insurance for your car and home: Amica, (800) 992-6422, www.amica.com; Colonial Penn, (800) 847-1729, www.geautoinsurance.com; Geico, (800) 841-3000, www.geico.com; USAA, (800) 531-8080, www.usaa.com; 21st Century, (800) 211-7233, www.21stcentins.com. Page 141.

Life insurance: SelectQuote, (800) 343-1985, www.selectquote.com; Termquote, (800) 444-8376, www.term-quote.com. Page 142.

InsWeb: www.insweb.com, page 142.

Internet Sites

10-K Wizard: www.10kwizard.com, page 38.

Bigcharts: www.bigcharts.com, page 82.

CBS MarketWatch: cbs.marketwatch.com, page 82.

ClearStation: www.clearstation.com, page 82.

iExchange: www.iexchange.com, page 82.

Jason Kelly: www.jasonkelly.com, page 83.

Morningstar: www.morningstar.com, page 83.

The Motley Fool: www.fool.com, page 83.

Multex: www.multex.com, page 84.

Raging Bull: www.ragingbull.com, page 84.

Smartmoney: www.smartmoney.com, page 84.

TheStreet.com: www.thestreet.com, page 84.

Worldlyinvestor: www.worldlyinvestor.com, page 85.

Yahoo Finance: finance.yahoo.com, page 85.

Long-Distance Phone Services

OneSuite.com: www.onesuite.com, page 141.

Magazines

SmartMoney: (800) 444-4204, www.smartmoney.com, page 81.

Worth: (800) 777-1851, www.worth.com, page 81.

Newsletters

The Chartist: (800) 942-4278, page 85.

Morningstar FundInvestor and **StockInvestor:** (800) 735-0700, www.morningstar.com, pages 85–86.

MPT Review: (800) 454-1395, www.mptreview.com, page 86.

The NeatSheet: (800) 339-5671, www.jasonkelly.com, page 86.

No-Load Fund Investor: (800) 252-2042, www.sheldonjacobs.com, pages 86–87.

The Outlook: (800) 852-1641, page 87.

The Value Line Investment Survey: (800) 833-0046, www.valueline.com, page 87.

Newspapers

Investor's Business Daily: 800-831-2525, www.investors.com, pages 80–81.

Securities and Exchange Commission

Securities and Exchange Commission: www.sec.gov, enforcement@sec.gov, page 38.

Software

Mutual Fund Expert: (800) 237-8400, www.mutualfundexpert.com, page 87.

Power Investor: (800) 477-7188, www.powerinvestor.com, page 88.